CONVERSATIONS WITH TIM INGOLD

CONVERSATIONS WITH TIM INGOLD

Anthropology, education and life

Tim Ingold, Robert Gibb, Philip Tonner
and Diego Maria Malara

First published in 2024 by
Scottish Universities Press
SUP Publishing CIC
International House
38 Thistle Street
Edinburgh
EH2 1EN

https://www.sup.ac.uk
Text © Tim Ingold, Robert Gibb, Philip Tonner and Diego Maria Malara 2024
Images © Copyright holders named in captions

This work is licensed under Creative Commons Attribution-NonCommercial 4.0 International licence. This licence enables reusers to distribute, remix, adapt, and build upon the material in any medium or format for noncommercial purposes only, and only so long as attribution is given to the creator. Attribution should include the following information:

Ingold, T., Gibb, R., Tonner, P. and Malara, D.M. 2024. *Conversations with Tim Ingold: Anthropology, education and life*. Glasgow, Scottish Universities Press.
https://doi.org/10.62637/sup.cmnz6231

Third-party materials are not covered by this licence.
Please see the individual credit lines in the captions for information on copyright holders.
To view a copy of this license, visit https://creativecommons.org/licenses/by-nc/4.0/

ISBN (Hardback:) 978-1-917341-03-5
ISBN (Paperback): 978-1-917341-00-4
ISBN (PDF): 978-1-917341-02-8
ISBN (EPUB): 978-1-917341-01-1
DOI: https://doi.org/10.62637/sup.cmnz6231

All external links included were live at the time of publication.

An electronic edition can be downloaded free of charge at
https://doi.org/10.62637/sup.cmnz6231
or scan the following QR code

This book has been through a rigorous peer review process to ensure that it meets the highest academic standards. A copy of the full SUP Peer Review Policy & Procedure can be found here: https://www.sup.ac.uk/peer-review

Typeset and designed by Palimpsest Book Production Limited, Falkirk, Stirlingshire
Cover design: Nicky Borowiec
Cover portrait: © Rudi Nofiandri taken from a photo of Tim Ingold © Serena Campanini

CONTENTS

Notes on authors	vii
Acknowledgements	ix
Introduction *Robert Gibb and Philip Tonner*	1
Conversation 1: Life and career	17
Conversation 2: Anthropology, ethnography, education and the university	63
Conversation 3: Environment, perception and skill	101
Conversation 4: Animals, lines and imagination	137
Conversation 5: Looking back and forward	175
Afterword *Tim Ingold*	203
References	211
Index	221

NOTES ON AUTHORS

Tim Ingold is Professor Emeritus of Social Anthropology at the University of Aberdeen. He has carried out fieldwork among Saami and Finnish people in Lapland, and has written on environment, technology and social organisation in the circumpolar North, on animals in human society and on human ecology and evolutionary theory. His more recent work explores environmental perception and skilled practice. Ingold's current interests lie on the interface between anthropology, archaeology, art and architecture. His recent books include *The Perception of the Environment* (2000), *Lines* (2007), *Being Alive* (2011), *Making* (2013), *The Life of Lines* (2015), *Anthropology and/as Education* (2018), *Anthropology: Why It Matters* (2018), *Correspondences* (2020), *Imagining for Real* (2022) and *The Rise and Fall of Generation Now* (2024). Ingold is a Fellow of the British Academy and the Royal Society of Edinburgh, and a Knight (First Class) of Order of the White Rose of Finland. In 2022 he was made a CBE for services to Anthropology.
    Webpage: https://www.timingold.com/

Robert Gibb teaches anthropology and sociology at the University of Glasgow. He has conducted anthropological research on the antiracist movement in France and on questions of translation and interpretation in the asylum process in France and Bulgaria. His most recent publications are 'Metaphors and practices of translation in anglophone anthropology' (*Social Science Information*, 2023) and 'Re-Learning Hope: On Alienation, Theory and the "Death" of Universities' (*The Sociological Review*, forthcoming).
    Webpage: https://www.gla.ac.uk/schools/socialpolitical/staff/robertgibb/

Philip Tonner is a Senior Lecturer in the School of Education at the University of Glasgow. He holds a PhD in Philosophy from the University of Glasgow, a DPhil in Archaeology from the University of Oxford, and a PGDE in education from the University of Strathclyde. His work explores themes at the intersection of philosophy, anthropology, archaeology and education. He is the author of three books, *Heidegger, Metaphysics and the Univocity of Being* (Continuum 2010), *Phenomenology Between Aesthetics and Idealism* (Noesis Press 2015) and *Dwelling: Heidegger, Archaeology, Mortality* (Routledge 2018).

Webpage: https://www.gla.ac.uk/schools/education/staff/philiptonner/

Diego Maria Malara is a Senior Lecturer in Social Anthropology at the School of Social and Political Sciences, University of Glasgow. He holds a PhD in Social Anthropology from the University of Edinburgh and has studied in Italy, Sweden and the UK. His research to date has focused on religion and politics in Ethiopia, specifically Ethiopian Orthodox Christianity. His publications explore themes including secrecy, kinship, healing, historicity, ethics, food, embodiment, religious pluralism and nationalism. He has recently edited special issues on 'Lenience in Systems of Religious Meaning and Practices' (*Social Analysis*) and 'Ethnographies of Ethiopian Orthodox Christianity' (*Northeast African Studies*), and co-authored a report entitled 'Religion in Contemporary Ethiopia: History, Politics and Inter-religious Relations' (Rift Valley Institute).

Webpage: https://www.gla.ac.uk/schools/socialpolitical/staff/diegomariamalara/

ACKNOWLEDGEMENTS

Robert Gibb, Diego Maria Malara and Philip Tonner are grateful to Tim Ingold for his willingness to be interviewed five times over a period of two years, and for his contribution to the work of editing and revising the transcribed conversations for publication.

Philip Tonner would like to thank William P. Tonner and Philip Wallace for their help with the transcription process. Particular thanks are due to William P. Tonner for his supportive role during this work. Philip would also like to thank Lynsey Tonner for her support during the Zoom interview process.

Diego Maria Malara wishes to express his gratitude to Fatima Raja for her valuable editorial guidance and for proofreading selected sections of the interviews he transcribed.

All four authors thank Dominique Walker and Gillian Daly at Scottish Universities Press for the information and guidance they kindly provided at regular intervals over a 15-month period. The book also benefitted from the comments on the initial proposal by two anonymous reviewers and members of SUP's Editorial Board. Funding to cover the production charge of the book was generously provided by the University of Glasgow Library.

INTRODUCTION

Robert Gibb and Philip Tonner

> **Summary:** In this chapter we provide a brief introduction to Ingold's work and to the rest of the book.[1] We highlight some of the key contributions Ingold has made to advancing thinking and research, not only within anthropology, but also in many other fields across the arts, humanities and natural sciences, and point to where these are discussed in the conversations that follow. In so doing, we consider how Ingold's ideas have changed over time, the place of empirical research in his work and influences on his recent work from outside anthropology. We also acknowledge anthropology's complicated history and discuss how in the subsequent conversations Ingold reflects on this. Finally, we present a rationale for the interview format and reflect on the processes involved in producing a book of this kind.

'. . . life is not confined within generations but forged in the collaboration of their overlap' (Ingold 2024: viii).

Tim Ingold is one of the world's leading anthropologists. Over the past five decades, he has not only advanced thinking and research within the discipline of anthropology but also made significant contributions to a wide range of debates in both the arts and humanities and the natural sciences. Characterised by a series of highly

---

[1] We are very grateful to Tim Ingold and Diego Maria Malara for their helpful comments on the first draft of this chapter.

original attempts to synthesise and develop ideas and concepts from an impressive variety of fields – notably anthropology, archaeology, evolutionary biology, ecological psychology, phenomenology, education, art and architecture – his work is innovative, accessible and thought-provoking. It offers an original perspective on, among other topics: human–animal relations; evolution and social life; the perception of the environment; technology and skill; the history and anthropology of lines; art and architecture as making and knowing; education and attention; anthropology and ethnography; creative practice and imagination; and what it means to be human.

Conversations with Tim Ingold: Anthropology, education and life provides a wide-ranging and readable account of Ingold's life and career in the form of a series of interviews he gave over a two-year period to three anthropologists based at the University of Glasgow: Robert Gibb, Diego Maria Malara and Philip Tonner. The interview format allows Ingold to present his ideas in his own words – highlighting in the process how engaging he is as a speaker and as a thinker – and to explore with the interviewers some of the key debates surrounding his work. The discussion covers the entirety of Ingold's career to date, from his earliest publications to his most recent collection of essays, *Imagining for Real* (2022a) and his latest book *The Rise and Fall of Generation Now* (2024).

The five interviews or conversations – the terms will be used interchangeably here – gathered in the present volume focus in turn on the following themes: 'Life and Career'; 'Anthropology, Ethnography, Education and the University'; 'Environment, Perception and Skill'; 'Animals, Lines and Imagination'; and 'Looking Back and Forward'. At the start of each conversation the reader will find a short paragraph which summarises the main topics covered therein. Each also concludes with a 'Further Reading' section, containing references to specific texts by Ingold and other scholars; this information is intended to help interested readers explore further the issues and debates reviewed in the chapter concerned. In fact, part of what prompted the three of us (Gibb, Malara and Tonner) to approach Ingold in the first place, with the idea of a series of interviews, chimed with a view expressed by the editors of a recent multidisciplinary collection devoted to his work, namely, that it 'deserves wider recognition and productive and critical engagement' (Porr and Weidtmann 2024: xiii). We hope that *Conversations with Tim Ingold* can play its own part in attracting further attention to his writing internationally, both within anthropology and in many other fields of study.

With this end in mind, what the interview-based chapters have in common, beyond the different thematic focus in each, is a concern to explore four key questions: (1) What are the most significant contributions Ingold has made to anthropology and to other disciplines in the arts and humanities and the natural sciences? (2) What are the key influences that have shaped his life and career? (3) What criticisms have been made of his work, and how has he responded to these? (4) What are the likely future directions his work will take? In the rest of this introduction, we highlight some of the most important answers to these questions that emerge over the course of the five conversations, before concluding with some brief comments on the process of producing a book such as this, based on a series of interviews. In an 'Afterword', Ingold offers some additional reflections of his own on these conversations.

· · ·

A recurrent feature of Ingold's career to date, which he talks about in the final conversation included here, has been the attempt to 'synthesise' anthropology with a range of different fields or disciplines: for example, evolutionary biology, ecological psychology, art, architecture and design, education. This has often involved challenging, and seeking to move beyond, binary distinctions such as between biology and culture, and between evolution and history, that are so characteristic of Western modernity (see the final section of Conversation 3). Similarly, in his most recent collection of essays (Ingold 2022a), Ingold tackles the opposition between 'imagination' and 'reality', as he discusses towards the end of Conversation 4. These are all exciting, thought-provoking contributions, which have attracted considerable attention and influenced debates not only within anthropology but also across the arts, humanities and natural and social sciences.

Given this sustained effort over many years to transcend disciplinary divisions and conceptual dichotomies, it might seem paradoxical that another of Ingold's major contributions has, at the same time, been his prominent role as a passionate advocate for the particular field of anthropology (for example, 2018a and b). How can these two, equally fundamental yet apparently conflicting aspects of his work be reconciled? The answer lies in the fact that what attracted Ingold to the subject in the first place, and has made him remain with it since, is his sense that 'anthropology is *constitutionally* in-between all the other disciplines'. He explains what he means by this in Conversation 2:

> The thing about anthropology, as we've always said, is that it doesn't concentrate on any particular slice of human life. Sociology deals with society; theology with religion; economics with the economy; politics with the state. But anthropology deals with the whole lot. It starts with humanity unsliced. And that, I think, is one of its great virtues.

Ingold is, of course, well aware of the discipline's complicated history, and he is very critical both in his published work and in these conversations (notably in Conversation 2) of how legacies from the colonial past continue to run through not just anthropology but academia more generally. In addition, he recognises that anthropologists have not been very successful in explaining to the general public why their discipline is so important, and that this has left it 'vulnerable institutionally' and subject to cuts during periods of contraction. One of the main underlying problems, he suggests, is that 'we have been less than clear in our own minds about the purpose of anthropology in today's world'. A contributing factor here, in his view, has been a growing tendency since the mid-1980s to reduce anthropology to ethnography. He has opposed this development (Ingold 2008, 2014a), for reasons discussed in the third section of Conversation 2.

Against this background, what in Ingold's view is the value and distinctiveness of anthropology? In several of his recent books (for example, Ingold 2018a, b), he has presented an original and provocative case for 'why anthropology matters', and this is a theme that runs through all the conversations assembled here. As he explains in Conversation 4, he has in general terms been 'trying to think of a different way of doing anthropology', one that builds on the discipline's key strengths. His starting point is the assertion that 'every way of life is itself an experiment in how to live', an attempt by a particular society or group of people to answer the fundamental human question: 'How *should* we live?' Ingold claims that anthropology is virtually the only discipline which is 'actually listening to people, interested in what they have to say, and anxious to learn from it', rather than simply treating it as data. In other words, it is – or should be – committed to 'taking others seriously', one aspect of which is thinking about what can be learned from their various experiments in living. As Ingold states in the fourth section of Conversation 2:

> If we go to study *with* other people, it is because they have wisdom and experience from which we could potentially learn; it might help us all, collectively, in our future endeavours. That's why we do anthropology, in my view.

From this perspective, anthropology is fundamentally a process of learning and education (see also Ingold 2018b). Elaborating on this point, he argues that for anthropologists:

> The first priority ... must be educational rather than ethnographic. We're not here to describe or catalogue other people's lives; we're here to open ourselves up to them. If we understand education in this sense, then that's what we do in anthropology. At least, it is what we *should* be doing; it should be our first priority.

According to Ingold, then, there is more to anthropology than the ethnographic documentation of particular ways of life, valuable though the latter can be; crucially, it is a form of education that is concerned with investigating 'the conditions and possibilities of human life' – past, present and future (see also Ingold 2018a: 8). As he puts it later in Conversation 2, anthropology 'offers the possibility to reflect seriously on the big questions of how to live in a way that engages with real life'. It can thus be said that one of the major promises of Ingold's work is nothing less than a revitalised philosophical anthropology, one that ventures out into the flow of the world and engages with the voices it hears there in order to explore possible answers to the question of how to live.

One further aspect of Ingold's general perspective on anthropology is worth highlighting here before we mention more briefly some of the specific issues and themes he discusses in the following conversations. Given his conceptualisation of anthropology as a form of education, it is perhaps not surprising that he views teaching as central to the discipline. In the final conversation he outlines his own approach to teaching and explains why he believes that 'teaching is an essential part of *doing* anthropology'. As the following extract makes clear, the reason why he attaches so much importance to teaching is directly related to his view of anthropology as a form of education that involves learning from the wisdom of others:

> What I've learned is that if we are going to study with people 'out there', to study their experiments in living . . . then we are under some sort of obligation, if we have been transformed by what we've learned, to give something back. How do we give things back? Not primarily through publication, but through teaching. . . . I feel really strongly about this. I think it is appalling that teaching is so often regarded as the delivery of second-hand goods. In some ways, it is the be-all-and-end-all of anthropology.

As Ingold points out, most anthropologists working in universities spend considerably more time teaching students in classrooms than they do carrying out research in the field. Even though it rarely receives the same amount of prominence as fieldwork, teaching,

Ingold believes, is a fundamental element of anthropological practice. In the final conversation, he provides fascinating insights into his own approach to, and experiences of, teaching.

Over the past five decades, Ingold has made numerous other original contributions, enhancing our knowledge and understanding concerning a wide range of questions. Many of these are discussed in this book. In Conversation 3, for example, Ingold talks about his influential collection of essays, *The Perception of the Environment* (2000/2011b), as well as his writing on 'the mycelial person', the dwelling perspective, landscape, anthropocentrism, materials and materiality, and technique and skill. A further three key themes are explored in Conversation 4: Ingold's long-standing interest in human–animal relations and his argument for an 'anthropology beyond humanity'; his fascinating work on 'the anthropological archaeology of the line' and subsequent development of the notion of 'correspondence'; and the focus in his most recent collection of essays on imagination and reality, creation and creativity, and the meaning of 'one-world anthropology'. In the conversations, Ingold is also asked about many other aspects of his work and career, including, to give just two final examples, how he set up an anthropology department at the University of Aberdeen and his views on matters of religious belief (see Conversations 2 and 4, respectively).

In mapping here how Ingold's major contributions to anthropology and many other fields are explored in the following five conversations, our aim has been to provide an initial overview of the book's contents. We hope these interviews will provide readers new to Ingold's work with a wide-ranging and accessible introduction to his key ideas and arguments, while giving those already familiar with his writing further insights into it. We will address the latter now by briefly indicating what these conversations tell us about the influences that have shaped Ingold's work over the years, and about his views today on some of the debates it has stimulated.

· · ·

The conversations included here explore both continuities and changes in Ingold's thinking over the five decades of his career to date. In the process, Ingold reflects on the various influences that have shaped the development of his ideas over this period. These range widely, and there is not space to mention all of them here. Nevertheless, some particularly important ones are worth highlighting. At the start of the very first conversation, Ingold discusses the influence of his parents, noting, for example, that what he absorbed as a child from observing his father's work as a mycologist at home undoubtedly lies behind his subsequent interest in lines and the notion of the 'mycelial person' (Ingold 2003, 2018c). He also explains that the anthropologists Keith Hart and Fredrik Barth were crucial influences during his undergraduate and postgraduate studies at the University of Cambridge in the late 1960s and early 1970s. In the years immediately following this, the early writings of Karl Marx played a significant role in helping Ingold develop his own ideas, as he outlines towards the end of the third conversation.

Surprisingly perhaps, the main intellectual influences on Ingold's work over the past four decades have come from outside his 'home' discipline. With the exception of the French archaeologist and ethnologist André Leroi-Gourhan, philosophers – including Henri Bergson, Maurice Merleau-Ponty and Susan Oyama – and psychologists – notably James Gibson – have been theoretical 'guiding lights' for him, more so than social anthropologists. Ingold offers an explanation for this in the final conversation, suggesting that 'from the mid-1980s onwards, anthropology began to turn in on itself', following the publication of *Writing Culture* (Clifford and Marcus, 1986) and the debates that ensued. 'And the more introverted it became,' he continues, 'the more it assumed an ethnographic and anti-theoretical posture.' As a result, in recent years 'the really interesting, exciting theoretical developments always seemed to be coming from somewhere else' – that is, from outside social anthropology, and this is reflected in the way he himself has taken inspiration from authors working mostly in other disciplines.

It remains the case, however, that more than any other, one particular group of social anthropologists have shaped Ingold's current thinking, namely, his PhD students. In the final conversation, he declares that so far as practitioners of his own discipline are concerned, over the past several decades, 'they are the people from whom I've learned the most, and most enjoyed working with'. For example, one of the reasons he became interested in the relationship between writing and musical notation, which he went on to explore in *Lines* (2007a), lay in his supervision of a doctoral student, Kawori Iguchi, who was researching Japanese traditional music (see the final section of Conversation 1). Ingold explains why he has learned so much from his supervisees: 'It's not just because of what they're thinking, but also because of what they're reading. You get to know work in all sorts of areas that you would otherwise have never encountered' (Conversation 5). This can be related, more generally, to Ingold's view of anthropology as a form of education, and also to his approach to teaching. Reflecting on the latter in the final conversation, he states that: 'To teach is to bring students along with you, as fellow travellers, on a journey of intellectual discovery which you undertake together.' Accompanying his doctoral students on their respective journeys has clearly taught Ingold much that has enhanced his own work.

Finally, these conversations also identify some of the other factors that have played a part in changing Ingold's ideas over time. In Conversation 1, he explains that after publishing *Evolution and Social Life* (Ingold 1986a) and *The Appropriation of Nature* (1986b), he concluded that his attempts in these books to combine social anthropology, respectively, with evolutionary biology and ecology had 'ended in failure'. What helped him find an alternative path forward was a suggestion from the ecological psychologist Edward Reed that he read the work of James Gibson. Invitations to deliver lecture series have stimulated his thinking in productive ways too. For example, being invited by the Society of Antiquaries of Scotland to give the 2003 Rhind Lectures subsequently led to the publication of his influential book *Lines: A Brief History* (2007a). Similarly, he developed his argument about 'anthropology as education' (Ingold 2018b) through an extensive engagement with John Dewey's

Introduction

writings, in the course of preparing the 2016 Dewey Lectures (see the final section of Conversation 2).

. . .

Ingold's work has been, and continues to be, the focus of lively debates not only in anthropology but also in many other disciplines (important recent contributions include Howes 2022; Kochan 2024; and Porr and Weidtmann 2024). It would have been impossible to cover the full range of these in the conversations collected together in the present volume. Nevertheless, the interviewers invite Ingold to respond to some of the key objections that have been levelled against his ideas and arguments over the years. To take two specific examples, he discusses some of the criticisms of his influential articles, 'The Temporality of Landscape' (1993) and 'Materials Against Materiality' (2007b) in the first and second sections of Conversation 3.

A recurrent criticism of Ingold's approach more generally, which has been levelled even by otherwise sympathetic commentators (for example, Hornborg 2018 and Howard 2018), is that it devotes insufficient attention to politics and political economy. To date, his fullest and most direct response to such criticism has been in an article published almost two decades ago (Ingold 2005). How does he view the matter today? The present conversations provide many valuable insights into Ingold's current assessment of this aspect of his own work, as well as into his practical involvement in institutional politics, notably at the University of Aberdeen, where he has worked since 1999.

The place of politics and political analysis in Ingold's work is explored at some length in the first section of Conversation 2. Ingold begins by acknowledging that he is 'often criticised for leaving politics out', and for failing to engage adequately with questions of political power. It is certainly the case, he admits, that the latter are rarely the explicit focus of his writing. Nevertheless, he goes on to insist that 'my work is *intensely* political, but the politics lies in the writing, in the arguing'. To illustrate this, he points to the ways he has challenged the claims of cognitive science and neo-Darwinian biology, fields that in his view are underpinned by, and help to reproduce, the power of neoliberal corporations and the state. As noted above, his work has sought to dissolve various dichotomies characteristic of Western modernity, such as biology versus culture, and evolution versus history; these interventions can also be considered highly political. The same can be said of his most recently published book (Ingold 2024), which proposes that how we think about generations is crucial to addressing climate change and other urgent contemporary issues.

When Ingold maintains that 'the politics lies in the writing', however, he is referring not only to the specific arguments he advances but also to *how* he writes. The effort he makes to write in a clear and accessible manner reflects his opposition to what he describes as 'scholarly gobbledygook' and the 'exclusionary' nature of much academic writing. This is related to a wider aim, which Ingold has stated in a recent publication and discusses in the second section of Conversation 2: 'to demolish the walls that divide the land of academia from the rest of the world, and to expose the conceit of its inhabitants – a conceit that lingers as an uncomfortable legacy from the colonial past – that they alone are equipped to tackle questions of so deep a nature as to elude ordinary folk' (2021a: 143). Ingold's participation in the 'Reclaiming Our University' movement at the University of Aberdeen, a fascinating account of which he provides in the final section of Conversation 2, is a further concrete example of his commitment to questioning and attempting to transform structures of academic power.

The present volume also throws valuable light on the series of significant but controversial interventions Ingold has made over the past decade in disciplinary debates about the relationship between anthropology, ethnography and participant observation. In the third section of Conversation 2 he summarises the arguments he has developed on this question and the concerns that prompted them. He acknowledges some of the difficulties inherent in clarifying the difference between anthropology and ethnography, including how to explain the nature of the discipline to outsiders, both members of the general public and those working in other fields. In the process, he also explains how he thinks 'research' and 'methods' should be understood, and comments on the effects of a professionalisation of research in recent decades that has led to an institutional preoccupation with 'research methods training'.

At several points in the conversations, Ingold also talks at some length about his own fieldwork in the early 1970s, as a doctoral student, with the Skolt Sámi in northeastern Finland. In the second section of Conversation 1 he explains how he ended up carrying out research there in the first place, before providing a detailed account of his fieldwork. He discusses key issues such as language learning, relationships with key interlocutors in the field, how he wrote field-notes (he describes how he analysed these in section 3 of Conversation 2) and the role played by his PhD supervisor, John Barnes. Reflecting on his fieldwork in Lapland, Ingold comments: 'I didn't think I was a very good fieldworker, and I've never been one of those whose passion is always to go back, to take every possible opportunity to return to the field.' In the final section of Conversation 5, he also talks about what he would do differently now if he were able to wind back the clock and conduct his first fieldwork again.

In this connection, a noteworthy observation about Ingold's work was made by one of the anonymous reviewers of the proposal for the present book, which we had submitted to the publishers. The reviewer commented that:

> Ingold has a complicated relationship with the idea and practice of ethnography. His own in-depth field experience is largely confined to the Skolt Lapps, and it has often puzzled me that in the rest of his career he rarely returns to the subject. There is an absence of immersive long-term fieldwork. Beyond the very early work, there are no detailed, systematic analyses of his own data.

Although the interviewers did not ask Ingold about this directly in their conversations, his answers to other questions throw valuable light on the issues identified by the reviewer. Looking back over his career in the final section of Conversation 5, for example, Ingold comments: 'Overall, I am not by any measure a field anthropologist', acknowledging that he has conducted 'very little' actual field research. He explains – and we will return to this below – that one of his main regrets is that he was never able to write up fully the subsequent fieldwork he conducted in Lapland in 1979–80, because he found himself 'drifting' into work of a more theoretical nature.

According to Ingold, his later interest in lines, paths, atmospheres and landscapes – decades after the publication of *The Skolt Lapps Today* (1976) – was nevertheless influenced in part by his early fieldwork experience in Lapland. He claims that:

> It is this kind of sensibility, which soaks into you without your realising it at the time, that then leads you to develop your ideas along particular lines. That, I think, is the real reason why fieldwork is so important. It isn't because of the data you collect and the study you might write up on the basis of them, but because of something deeper that sinks in and affects the way you live your life, including scholarship.

Even though Ingold felt that his PhD thesis failed to capture 'the feel of the place' where he had conducted fieldwork, he suggests that the experience of inhabiting a particular kind of northern landscape, where each human and animal path has a history, fostered a sensibility that remained with him and has helped to shape his subsequent work.

Taken together, Ingold's reflections on his own fieldwork experience suggest a way of understanding how the different pieces of the 'puzzle' described by the reviewer cited above relate to each other. An additional element is provided by the very last exchange in these conversations, where he answers a question about his plans for the future. As Ingold explains, his immediate task was to complete work on an edited collection and a single-authored book. Both of these have since been published (Ingold 2022a, b), as has a further book (Ingold 2024). His intention after that, he tells us, is to return to Lapland and to resume the fieldwork he started there in 1979–80, but was unable subsequently to write up properly. These conversations therefore end at a point of new beginnings for Ingold: 'Having said all these things about ethnography . . . I shall nevertheless reinvent myself as an ethnographer again!' It will be fascinating to follow how this next stage of his life and career develops.

. . .

In his most recent book, *The Rise and Fall of Generation Now*, Ingold encourages us to think of generations as more like overlapping, entwined threads in a rope than as discrete layers stacked one on top of the other (2024: 1–5). He also uses the metaphor of the rope to understand academic fields of study, such as anthropology, writing that: 'Every discipline so named is a lineage of begetting, wound like a rope from the overlapping scholarly lives of its numerous practitioners' (2024: 112–13). In a similar way, the present volume can be viewed as the result of a collaboration that brought together four anthropologists from different but overlapping generations in a series of five conversations. As will be apparent from comments in several of these, it did so during the Covid-19 pandemic: the first interview took place on 9 October 2020 and the final one on 13 May 2022.

For each interview/conversation, Gibb, Malara and Tonner prepared a list of questions, compiled from suggestions they had made individually (shaped in part by their own respective intellectual interests), and sent this to Ingold in advance. They then asked him these questions in a video meeting on Zoom, and he responded, his answers sometimes leading to additional 'follow-up' questions and discussion of themes not covered by the interviewers' initial questions. All the interviews were recorded. The interviewers transcribed them and produced an initial edited version of each conversation. The latter was sent to Ingold, along with the full unedited transcript of the interview, to which he added more editing of his own and corrected some transcription errors. The interviewers then reviewed the amended version and made any final editorial changes they considered appropriate.

In response to the opening question of the very first conversation, Ingold notes that being interviewed has sometimes helped him to clarify his own thinking. An interview can be extremely useful too, we believe, for readers interested in learning more about a particular scholar and their work. The question-and-answer format lends itself to an engaging and accessible presentation of key ideas and arguments. Previous interviews with Ingold published in academic journals, such as those we've mentioned in the 'Further Reading' section at the end of Conversation 1, illustrate this very well. What is distinctive about *Conversations with Tim Ingold* is the enhanced breadth and depth of discussion made possible by a book-length volume in which no fewer than five interviews, each with a different thematic focus, are included. As the reader will discover, these conversations range widely, exploring in some detail not only Ingold's original contributions to anthropology and many other fields over the past five decades, but also his early life, undergraduate and postgraduate studies and subsequent academic career.

As Ingold has argued, anthropologists 'study *with* people, rather than making studies *of* them' (2018a: 11, italics in original). We suggest, finally, that therein also lies part of the rationale for this book of conversations with Ingold himself. Anthropology requires of us that we re-learn how to look at the world from within so that we might be able to express something of its very becoming. A conversational approach provides opportunities for this. A true conversation is a listening participation in emergence that is open to the future of what we might become. This is what we have attempted to pursue in the conversations that follow.

CONVERSATION 1:

Life and career

> **Summary:** This is an edited version of a wide-ranging interview that Gibb, Malara and Tonner conducted with Ingold about his life and career on 9 October 2020. It covers in turn Ingold's childhood and school experiences, his undergraduate and postgraduate studies and his academic career at the universities of Manchester and Aberdeen. Ingold reflects on the influences that have shaped his personal and intellectual development and how his interests have evolved over this time. A fascinating account in itself, this also helps to situate the specific themes explored in the subsequent conversations in the wider context of Ingold's life, and of an academic career spanning five decades.

Robert Gibb

First of all, Tim, thank you very much for agreeing to this series of interviews, just as you've previously agreed to be interviewed by other colleagues from around the world, working not only in anthropology but also in other fields and disciplines. When did you start receiving interview requests?

Tim Ingold

I don't remember exactly. Over the last three or four years maybe, but not much before then. It is true that they've multiplied over the last few years. Most often correspondents email questions to which I then respond. It's more usual for me to do it in that way than directly, as we are doing now. I don't accept all such requests. But if the interviewers are serious and have really good things to talk about, then I have often found it quite helpful for clarifying my own ideas. It helps to have someone pose a question which you are compelled to answer, and it can sometimes be quite challenging. It's been of great benefit to me.

(A) CHILDHOOD AND SCHOOL EXPERIENCES

Philip Tonner

Please can you tell us where you were born and about your parents and grandparents.

Tim Ingold

I was born in 1948, in a small town called Sevenoaks in the county of Kent, in southeast England. My father was a botanist; his specialism was mycology, the study of fungi. When I was born, he had already taken up a post at Birkbeck College, London, where he was Professor of Botany. My mother was trained as a geologist, but in those days it wasn't easy for a married woman to have a career, so basically she was at home, looking after me and my three elder sisters. My eldest sister is 13 years older; the next one, eight years older; and the next one, five years older. So I turned up as very much the youngest in the family. And of course, that was soon after the end of the Second World War. It was the period of the postwar baby boom. I don't remember very much about my grandparents. I didn't get to know my two grandfathers at all. Of my two grandmothers, one was enormous fun, but the other I remember as stern and bedridden.

Philip Tonner

Where did you go to school and what subjects did you study in secondary school?

Tim Ingold

My parents sent me to what was called a preparatory school – meaning a private, single-sex primary school – which was run by a gentleman in a splendid country mansion. It was mostly a happy place, though looking back, I do wonder about one particular teacher, not to mention the gentleman-headmaster's predilection for the cane, weakly administered to the hand, or occasionally the backside, of any miscreant pupil. Then they sent me to Leighton Park School, which is also a public (meaning private, fee-paying) school, situated on the outskirts of Reading. I have never quite forgiven my parents for this, because I was only 11 when I was packed off from home, and the early years of boarding were really hard. Once I'd got through the worst of the teenage years and had reached the top (sixth) form, the independence from home was wonderful, but up until then it was awful. I was bullied a lot, and sometimes caused consternation by walking in my sleep in the dormitory. Because I was considered clever, they bumped me up by one year. That made it even more difficult because most of my classmates were a year older than me, and that makes a big difference when you're 13 or 14. It meant that I took what were called O levels in those days – that is, ordinary level exams – when I was only 14. I then went straight into Advanced level, and it was simply assumed that since I was good at maths and science, I would take maths and science subjects. I never really thought twice about it. I took my A-level exams in mathematics, advanced mathematics, physics and chemistry, when I was 16. I was still very immature, having led a thoroughly sheltered life. I had no idea about the world or about anything, really, and there I was, already slated to be a scientist. I took a year off in between school and university, but then started off at university studying natural science.

Philip Tonner

How formative do you think your childhood and school experiences were for your subsequent career and intellectual projects?

Tim Ingold

That's hard to say. Family experiences were probably more formative than school experiences: things like going for walks in the countryside, and topics discussed around the dinner table at home. I think these affected me more than anything I did at school. But I'm not sure; it was all so long ago! I am in no doubt, however, that my father had an extremely strong influence on how I think. I had a wonderfully happy home. Both my parents were amazing. My mother gave me all the stability one could possibly ask for, so I could feel safe and secure, and my father gave me a sense of intellectual curiosity and rigour. Putting the two together, I couldn't really have asked for better parents.

Diego Maria Malara

Could you elaborate a bit more on what these conversations were about, what the intellectual climate at home was, and more specifically how your parents influenced your thinking?

Tim Ingold

My dad, as I mentioned, was a mycologist. There's something about fungi – I mean, fungi are very curious organisms! They don't behave as organisms should. My dad was completely in love with these fungi, and his approach to studying them was very innovative for its time. He was one of the first, in the early 1930s, to insist on the importance of field experience in botanical education. Until then, students would simply encounter pickled, preserved specimens of plants or fungi in a laboratory. My dad was the one who said: 'You cannot possibly understand a fungus unless you go into the woods, find it, see where it's growing, what it's doing with everything else.' It seems obvious now, but at the time, it was revolutionary. He would sometimes bring his students to our house for fungal forays and they'd all go wandering in the woods and come back and have tea at home and discuss what they'd found. I was a little boy observing all these things going on around me. Here was a group of grown-ups who were completely fascinated by these odd things that crop up in the forest. I couldn't help but absorb some of this atmosphere. So that was one thing.

The second thing was that my dad's specialism was not in fact the fungi you find growing in the woods, but microscopic fungi known as aquatic hyphomycetes. There's actually a genus of *Ingoldia* fungi, named after him! My dad was especially interested in the mechanisms by which these fungi contrived to discharge their spores. He would observe this going on under the microscope, in real time. He could practise this kind of science and make genuinely new discoveries without needing a fancy lab; indeed, he did a lot of his work on our dining-room table. He would find the fungi by going for walks along the river bank, take a few glass tubes with him, fill up the glass tubes with mucky water from the side of the stream, bring it home, put it under the microscope and discover all these marvellous organisms. There he would be, sitting with a mapping pen, Indian ink and Bristol board, drawing what he saw – very, very carefully and very beautifully. It was obvious to all of us that he was completely besotted with his fungi. But he was a very rational, empirical man, who refused to admit to his feelings for what he studied. He would say: 'I'm just a scientist. I'm observing. I don't talk about love. That's got nothing to do with it.' But we all knew that this is really what it was. As a child, watching him at work, I must have absorbed a certain attitude towards lines and drawing, and towards the curiously reticular nature of fungi.

Life and career

My dad could never understand anthropology or why I should want to study it. Half a century later, when I wrote my book about lines and gave him a copy to read, he said: 'I have no idea what all this is about.' I tried to tell him: 'Well, look, your fungi are right there, at the heart of it.'

The other thing I loved, when I was a boy, was trains. I spent a lot of time trainspotting on station platforms, and built a model railway. I would go for walks in the countryside and take black-and-white photographs with the sort of Kodak camera you could buy in those days, and make drawings of interesting buildings. Then I would use the photos and drawings to make miniature-scale models, which I included in the railway layout. This too was very important, because through photographing and model-making you develop an eye for landscape and for buildings. My mother was my main supporter in all this railway modelling, whereas my dad wasn't interested in it at all.

These were very strong influences. The conversations we would have around the dinner table were about modern art, politics and religion, of which I had zero understanding at the time. One of my elder sisters had taken up painting; another was very active in the communist students' movement. My dad was a fervent atheist, but my mum wasn't quite so sure. So there would be lots of very vigorous conversations around things like that. My main problem was that I was always being left out. I wanted to talk about my trains, but I could never get a word in edgeways because my sisters would be having these intense arguments about art, politics and religion that I didn't understand.

(B) UNDERGRADUATE AND POSTGRADUATE STUDIES

Robert Gibb

What did you do in your year out between secondary school and university?

Tim Ingold

Technically, it was nine months: I still spent the final autumn at school to take the Cambridge entrance exams. Then I left. I worked in a supermarket for a bit, unloading lorries and stocking shelves, before travelling to Finland. That was my first trip to Finland. I travelled north through the country, through Lapland, and even visited the place where I would eventually carry out fieldwork. I had seen an advertisement for student labour to work on farms in Norway. I applied, and was given a placement on a farm on the coast of northern Norway, in a little village called Alstahaug, near the town of Sandnessjøen. I decided that to get to this place, I may as well travel through Finland. I had just been to see the film *Dr Zhivago*, newly released, and had been especially captivated not only by its heroine, played by Julie Christie, but also by some of the railway scenes, filmed along a line in Finnish Karelia. I imagined Finland as a country of wood-burning locomotives and girls as beautiful as Julie Christie! I was also very much attracted to the idea of the North. My family home was full of books about the North because both my parents were rather keen on it, although they didn't travel north themselves. I worked on this farm for a couple of months and then came home again. That was my period in between. It introduced me to Finland and to a part of the world that was subsequently to become of great importance in my life.

Robert Gibb

You'd applied to do science at Cambridge?

Tim Ingold

Yes, without even thinking about it. It was just an assumption on everybody's part that I would read natural sciences, because I'd done the standard Advanced level exams required for it: maths, further maths, physics and chemistry. I gave no real thought to the matter of what I should be doing until long after I arrived at university. I went to study natural sciences, and that was that.

At Cambridge, the quality of teaching was dreadful. You'd be sitting there, in a pretty large class, in a big, old lecture theatre, and some Nobel prize-winning scientist would be standing, usually with his back to the audience, writing stuff on the blackboard in chalk, which we then all had to copy down. And that was it! There was no sense of critical engagement, no discussion, nothing. I was massively disillusioned by the whole thing. At that time, the Vietnam War was at its height and there were big protests going on, including a campaign for social responsibility in science, which I joined. Though I was not really politicised, I did get the sense that something was seriously wrong with science, and that our teachers were being utterly complacent about it. I never reacted against science itself, but I did come to the conclusion, by the end of my first year at university, that there was no way I could be a professional scientist. I was disillusioned less with science itself than with what had happened to it. I was appalled not only by the way it was taught, but also by the way in which it had allowed itself to be co-opted by the military-industrial complex, as we would call it now. With the Vietnam War going on, this was very much 'in your face'.

That was the first year. I had to decide what to do next, so I browsed through the *Cambridge University Reporter*, a kind of gazetteer that lists all the possible courses you can take. I was looking for something that would bridge the gap between the natural sciences and the humanities, while at the same time remaining close to real life. I found two possible alternatives: one was the history and philosophy of science and the other was anthropology. My dad happened to know the anthropologist Jean La Fontaine, because they'd both been teaching at Birkbeck, before Jean moved to the London School of Economics. He arranged for me to go and meet Jean and talk about anthropology and, as I recall, she was very helpful. She told me that I should read Fredrik Barth's book, originally published in 1959, *Political Leadership Among Swat Pathans*. I read it, and that was it! I was bowled over by the book, and decided there and then that I would read anthropology, and not the history and philosophy of science.

Here, I thought, is a discipline that really does bridge the divide between the sciences and the humanities, while also staying close to life. That's why I chose it. I was allowed to retake the first year, which meant that I did all three years of the Archaeological and Anthropological Tripos, as it was then called. The first year included courses in Archaeology, Physical Anthropology and Social Anthropology, and at the end of the year we had to choose which line to take. I chose Social Anthropology, which at that time was blessed with a fiery lecturer who got everyone excited, namely Edmund Leach. Leach was keen on introducing the structuralist approach of Claude Lévi-Strauss to British anthropology, so we students heard quite a lot about this, and found it super-interesting. It appealed to me as a kind of pure mathematics of social life. My other lecturers were Meyer Fortes, Jack Goody and, for a while, Ray Abrahams. Their styles of lecturing were, respectively, monotonous, chaotic and dull. The person who inspired me most, however, was Keith Hart, who had been doing fieldwork in northern Ghana with the Tallensi people whom Fortes had studied earlier. Keith was my supervisor in that second year, and he basically taught me how to write. He could be ruthlessly critical without ever being dismissive – an excellent guide and a wonderfully intelligent person to argue with.

These, in the late 1960s, were the last days of structural-functionalism, so our bible was A. R. Radcliffe-Brown's *Structure and Function in Primitive Society*, a collection of essays dating from 1952. My own copy of the book had originally belonged to one of my elder sisters, to whom it had been presented as a school prize in 1958! Nobody reads the book nowadays, but we all had to learn it virtually by heart. At that time, however, British structural-functionalism was under fire from the new-fangled structuralism coming in from France, led by Lévi-Strauss. Fortes was on the side of structural-functionalism and Leach on the side of French structuralism – although having originally been trained as an engineer, Leach was keen to convert Lévi-Strauss's rather abstract, quasi-geometrical structures into systems that actually worked. Goody was somewhere in the middle, developing his own ideas, which were something else again. At that time, also, transactionalism, pioneered by the Norwegian anthropologist Fredrik Barth, was making its mark as a possible successor to structural-functionalism, and I was very attracted to it. Indeed, I was so taken with Barth's ideas that I would later go on to study with him in Norway.

Assuming that I would go on to postgraduate study, I then had to decide where to do my field research. By that stage I'd resolved that I wanted to work in Lapland, in the very community I had visited on my first trip through Finland. The Department had no idea how to deal with this, because most students carried out their fieldwork in formerly British colonies, mainly in Africa, India or southeast Asia. They could not understand how anybody would want to do their fieldwork somewhere in the north.

The thing was that at the end of my first year of anthropology, in summer 1968, I had found myself back in Finland. I had joined what in Britain was called Voluntary Service Overseas (VSO): you would sign up, and then be sent off to a summer workcamp somewhere. It was a great way of meeting people from different countries and of doing something useful at the same time. But you had to go where you were told. It just happened, by pure chance, that I was told to go to a place in Karelia, in eastern Finland, to help with the harvest. There were many farms there with big families in which the male head of the household had passed away, usually due to heart disease. Mortality from heart disease was especially high in rural Finland, especially among middle-aged men, due in part to a diet heavy in saturated fats, but in part, also, to the long-term health effects of wartime hardships. A lot of women were therefore having to manage their farms, with their children still too small for heavy work. We went to help with the haymaking. We had a fabulous time, and formed many friendships there that have remained with us for the rest of our lives.

I was one of the first to arrive, and was immediately set to work peeling potatoes for dinner. On the opposite side of the potato bucket was a girl from the western side of Finland, and it was immediately apparent to this girl, whose name was Anna, that I had absolutely no idea how to peel potatoes. I'd probably never peeled potatoes in my life! But we ended up having many long walks and conversations, and continued to correspond by mail after the camp was over. Then, the year after that, she and I together ran a similar workcamp in Sevettijärvi, in the very place in Lapland where I would later go on to do my fieldwork. The local building inspector had decided that the Skolt Sámi people, who were living there, ought to eat more potatoes, and our task was to build semi-subterranean, concrete cellars, in which potatoes could be preserved from frost over the winters. Most of these cellars, though now put to other uses, are still standing. During that time, I got to know many of the people in the Skolt community. That was the obvious reason why, when it came to deciding where to do fieldwork, I resolved to go there. At that time, moreover, Anna was studying in Turku, in southwestern Finland, so she could be with me, during university vacations, in the field. She is still with me now, my wife of fifty-one years and counting!

So that's how it happened. In those days, research grants were relatively easy to obtain. I received a studentship from the College, because I'd got a First Class degree, as well as a studentship from what was then called the Social Science Research Council,[1] and I was able to combine the two. So funding was not a problem. But the Cambridge department was a bit stuck as to whom to appoint to supervise my PhD, because they had no-one with expertise in that area. In the end they settled on John Barnes. John had just

---

1   In the United Kingdom, state support for research is primarily delivered through the research councils, and research in social anthropology came under the remit of the Social Science Research Council (SSRC), founded in 1965. Subsequently, in 1983, it was renamed the Economic and Social Research Council (ESRC), on the instigation of Conservative government ministers for whom the economy naturally took precedence over society, and who could not countenance the idea that the study of society could ever be scientific.

been appointed, in 1969, to the newly created Chair of Sociology at the University of Cambridge. The Chair had been established in the face of strong resistance from dons who refused to recognise sociology as a legitimate subject of study, and the issue had been resolved, in typical Cambridge style, by appointing a social anthropologist rather than a sociologist to the post! John had worked mostly in Central Africa, but had also done some fieldwork in Papua New Guinea. But apart from his work in Africa and PNG, John had also spent some time in Norway, on a little island quite close to the city of Bergen, called Bremnes, and had used this work to develop what was called 'social network theory'.

Thus, when I began my doctoral research in 1970, John became my official supervisor, and for me he was perfect. He didn't really do anything much. I saw him before I went to the field; I saw him again when I had my complete PhD; he turned up once in the field itself, when we got him to help mend the roof of the cabin where we were staying and dig a waste pit. And I will always remember the dark midwinter's night when one of my Sámi neighbours knocked on the door of our cabin, bearing a mystery package. When I opened it, I found a copy of John's book, just published, *Three Styles in the Study of Kinship*. It was the sheer incongruity of this incident that stayed in my mind. John was the nicest of men; he and his wife Frances became good friends. And he sometimes helped with practical questions to which I didn't know the answer – for example, when I first thought I'd try to submit an article to the journal of the Royal Anthropological Institute, then called *Man*. The journal's instructions for authors said that you had to submit your manuscript on 'A4 or foolscap paper, double-spaced'. I had no idea what all that meant. Nobody had told me about A4 or foolscap, or explained the meaning of single-spaced and double-spaced. John could answer questions like these, which was really helpful. But I also had an unofficial supervisor in Fredrik Barth. After an autumn in Cambridge, I went off to Bergen and worked with Fredrik in the Bergen department for a term before I left to the field. And I spent another term there after my return from the field, following which I went back to Cambridge.

Diego Maria Malara

Who were the students you discussed anthropology with and how did these discussions shape your own approach to anthropology?

Tim Ingold

During that time, while I was a research student at Cambridge, I didn't talk much with anybody. I remember having lots of discussions with my fellow students in Bergen, because they were all followers of Fredrik Barth, and all heavily into transactionalism, which, for me too at the time, seemed to be the answer to everything. Fredrik was incredibly charismatic, and one only had to be in his circle to become a follower. Thus, prior to my departure for the field, I thought of myself as a Barthian, as a transactionalist. But when I returned, a year and a half later, transactionalism was dead and the new thing was neo-Marxism, recently arrived from France. In Cambridge, I found myself in a complete bubble, like most PhD students there. People tell me that it is little better today – that Cambridge is still full of people writing doctoral theses, sitting in libraries, or in lofts, or rooms somewhere, working away in almost total isolation, with almost no-one remotely interested in their existence. That's certainly how it was for me. No-one seemed to care that I existed at all. As a doctoral student, you were supposed to attend the weekly Social Anthropology seminar. But the seminar had a fixed seating plan in which all the important people sat around the central table, and all the research students around the edge of the room. You wouldn't dare ask a question until those around the table had asked their questions first. It was certainly not the most inspiring of academic environments in which to work. In fact, I remember it as a time of great intellectual isolation, which only ended when I finally arrived in Manchester.

The idea that students should be trained in fieldwork, that they should spend a year on research training before they can even think about going to the field – all that came later. I know that for many students nowadays, this can be deeply frustrating. The pendulum has swung from one extreme to the other, from there having been no training at all – when it was just assumed that you would muddle through – to there being far too much, forcing students to spend ages being trained in techniques which will likely be of no conceivable use to them. It's annoying because it gets in the way: when students should really be spending time learning the language or languages they will need to speak in the field, for example, they're having to practise multivariate statistics. It's really unhelpful. But I don't think I received any training in fieldwork, nor did anybody else at that time.

Robert Gibb

What language learning did you undertake for fieldwork?

Tim Ingold

I had to learn Finnish. I should have systematically learnt the Skolt Sámi language, but I didn't. My teacher in Finnish was my future wife, Anna. She was a very strict and demanding teacher! Finnish is not an easy language, but I found that once I'd got the hang of the basic grammar, and once I was actually there in the country and having to use it every day, it came pretty quickly. I needed to be fluent in Finnish to be able, obviously, to talk to Finns, as well as to read the literature, newspapers, archives and documents of all sorts. That was essential. In the field, the people themselves were speaking a mixture of Finnish and Skolt Sámi. Though I've forgotten most of it now, I did pick up a bit of Sámi. I could roughly follow what people were talking about, but could not really speak it myself. I never sat down to learn it systematically, and that was definitely a shortcoming. In retrospect, I should have done that. But one of the difficulties in doing so is that it is rather difficult to learn two closely related languages, like Finnish and Sámi, at the same time. You get interference effects. Coping with both languages was simply too much, although in hindsight I should have made the effort. But I didn't. For most practical purposes, I got by with Finnish. But that's partly because my study was focused on what we would now consider a rather traditional theme: it was a study of social organisation. I wasn't dealing with myths or ritual or storytelling or folklore or poetry or placenames or landscape. I wish now that I had addressed these themes! To do so I would have had to learn the language. But in those days, it was not on the agenda. Social anthropological research, then, meant studying kinship, local-level politics, economic life, that sort of thing.

Philip Tonner

What was your first fieldwork like? You've already spoken about this a little, but would you like to elaborate?

Tim Ingold

I was there in the first instance for 16 months, from May 1971 to September 1972. So, it ran over spring, summer, autumn and winter, and back to spring and summer again. I started off living in a tent in the yard of a family that I had got to know from my previous visit. Then I found out there was a cabin going spare which I could rent, and I lived there. Finally, we had to move to another empty cottage, when the owner of the cabin – a Finnish labourer who had married a Skolt woman – wanted it back. So, apart from that first month or two, I was looking after myself in my own place. One of the difficulties or oddities of doing fieldwork in a place like this is that there are so few people. The community I was studying had a population of just over three hundred, spread over a vast area. It's not like sitting in the middle of a village and watching life going on around you; you have to find the people, and finding them can sometimes be pretty difficult.

Over the summer, for example, people go off to fishing cabins that are dotted all around a vast landscape. To reach them you might have to hike for twenty kilometres through the forest, and then you might find them or you might not. I remember that one of the things I had to cope with during fieldwork, from time to time, was intense loneliness. I could be on my own for quite long periods. That's life up there, and people get used to being on their own, but for me, it was one of those things I had to learn. And I found out lots of things about myself in the process. Not much happened. Life, for a lot of the time, was pretty dull. I remember thinking, many times, 'What am I doing here? Days are just passing, with absolutely nothing going on. I'm stuck here in this place, while somewhere beyond the horizon, life must be happening.' I didn't think I was a very good fieldworker, and I've never been one of those whose passion is always to go back, to take every possible opportunity to return to the field. I was quite glad to finish it off.

Figure 1
Tim Ingold with Enoch, his neighbour's tame reindeer
(Sevettijärvi, Finland, summer 1971) © Tim Ingold

But my 16 months in the field was also, in many ways, an incredible experience, and I would not have missed it for anything. I certainly didn't envy my contemporaries in other fields of study, buried deep in libraries or archives, 'moving bones', as someone once said of doctoral research, 'from one graveyard to another'. By comparison, my life as a researcher, largely lived in the open air, was full of adventure. I was still so young – just twenty-three or twenty-four – and still growing up, so the experience literally changed me. I discovered quite a lot about who I thought I was. But it's the same for everyone else who has carried out fieldwork. It is potentially transformative for anyone who undertakes it, and it certainly was for me. Afterwards, colleagues would ask: 'How on earth could you go there? It must have been so cold!' There were contemporaries of mine who had done fieldwork in India or Africa, for example, and had contracted every illness under the sun. They had spent much of their time in the field suffering from one bug after another, from dysentery to malaria, yet they would still ask of me: 'How did you manage when it was so cold?' But if it's cold, you just put on more clothes until you're warm enough. There may have been lots of mosquitoes in the summer months, but none of them carried malaria. I never suffered from dysentery. On the whole, it was a pretty healthy place to work.

Diego Maria Malara

Can you reflect on how the peculiarity of your research in Lapland shaped the ways in which you came to see anthropology and your attention to specific themes, such as the atmosphere, lines, trails, landscape and so on?

Tim Ingold

It definitely had an influence. But the odd thing is that in my thesis, and in the book based on it, this doesn't show at all. In writing up, I brought in lots of detailed analysis about economic life, householding, kinship, local politics and the rest of it. Yet all the experience of life, the feel of the place, seemed to vanish as through a sieve. I remember feeling very disappointed that in the kind of thesis I was supposed to write, I could capture none of this. Yet it is precisely what passed through the sieve of analysis that has stayed with me, long after I had forgotten all the details. It was only later on, really, that I began to think about why I was becoming so interested in lines, paths, atmospheres, landscapes. It must have come partly from childhood experience, but also partly from fieldwork.

It is this kind of sensibility, which soaks into you without your realising it at the time, that then leads you to develop your ideas along particular lines. That, I think, is the real reason why fieldwork is so important. It isn't because of the data you collect and the study you might write up on the basis of them, but because of something deeper that sinks in and affects the way you live your life, including scholarship. If you're working in the North, there's something about those northern landscapes. One thing is that whenever you're walking through or following a path of some kind – it might be an animal or a human path – that path has a history. As you go along you see the remains of old fireplaces, each with its stories, of things that happened here and there. You cannot inhabit this kind of landscape without beginning to think of life as something that happens along pathways.

This is how Sámi people think, as a matter of course. People *are* their lines in the landscape. It's just obvious; it goes without saying. It's the same when it comes to things like weather and atmosphere. You cannot help but soak these up. There's something about the immensity of a northern landscape, of its summer light and winter darkness. I've called it an *intimate immensity*, the feeling of a world which is very, very huge but at the same time very, very close. It is rather special to northern landscapes. You don't find it elsewhere, and it does shape the way you think and feel. It is about seasonality, about long hours of darkness, long hours of daylight. These sorts of things really do affect the way you think. This is not to say that environment determines thought, but it does mean that somehow the landscape you're in, and the people inhabiting that landscape, get inside you and shape the way you think and feel. That's certainly what happened with me.

Diego Maria Malara

We often ask people what influence specific teachers had on them, but we seldom ask about the influence of one's interlocutors in the field. I was wondering who, among your interlocutors, had the greatest impact on you and why?

Tim Ingold

Well, there was a particular man who, for most of my fieldwork in Lapland, was my next-door neighbour. His place was just up the road from the cabin where I was staying. He was called Piera Porsanger. He would have been 48 years old when I was in the field at around 23 years old, so he was 25 years older than I. Piera was a real philosopher but a hopeless reindeer herder, so his family was very poor. He had lost most of his herd. He had an enormous wife and lots of children who were always round at my place, ever inquisitive and asking about things. They were hyper-intelligent children. Piera spoke five languages fluently: Finnish, Norwegian and three kinds of Sámi. He was himself a Mountain Sámi and his wife was a Skolt Sámi. He was just immensely curious about everything. He was short, thin, wiry, myopic and wore thick spectacles. But what a brilliant mind he had! I remember him talking about one of the big issues during my fieldwork, concerning the construction of reindeer fences. There was an intense argument about where to build these fences, particularly a new fence to be built between the territories of two neighbouring reindeer-herding associations. But Piera told the story from the perspective of a reindeer. This reindeer is following his usual route, and comes up against this fence. And he says to himself: 'Where the hell do I go from here?' It somehow captured the whole thing. Piera is thinking of his animals and wondering:

'Where am I supposed to go with this fence in the way?' It just resonates.

Then there was the elderly couple with whom I first stayed when I arrived, Pekka and Liisa Feodoroff. Liisa was a powerful and outspoken woman, but Pekka was a small, mild and rather shy man, very much dominated by his overbearing wife. But they always used to tell of how, as a young man, Pekka crossed the newly drawn international frontier between Finland and Russia in order to rescue his future wife from behind the lines and bring her back. It's a great story of kidnapping. There were lots of stories like that from the field.

Diego Maria Malara

You said that you saw your supervisor before you left and then when your thesis was basically written. I suppose you submitted a draft for him to read, right?

Tim Ingold

Yes, more or less. So perhaps I was not quite fair to suggest that John, my supervisor, never looked at it until it was finished. I did see him on other occasions, but not really to go through the material in any depth. Put it this way: I was quite happy to do my own thing, and I didn't really want to have somebody poking their nose into everything I was doing or everything I was writing. So, from my point of view, it was fine. I could just get on with it, knowing he was always there in case I needed help with any practical questions. He was very supportive in that way; I felt I had someone in whom I could completely trust, someone I knew was always there for me if I needed.

I wrote my fieldnotes in four copies. I had used very thin paper, with carbon paper in between, so that I could write a top copy and instantly produce three additional copies. I would send the bottom copy periodically in the post back to John, as an insurance in case I lost everything else. So I thought of John, in some ways, as a backup. But he also used to ask very practical and occasionally odd questions. I remember talking, for example, about how Sámi people would send joints of frozen reindeer meat to relatives who had left to live in the cities down south, and his immediate response was to ask what happened in the post when the meat began to melt. I had never thought of that! Where necessary, he could also pull a few strings. For example, he managed to fix it for me to attend the Decennial Conference of the Association of Social Anthropologists, held in Oxford in 1973. In those days PhD students were definitely not welcome at professional anthropology conferences, but he managed to smuggle me in and, as a result, I was able to meet a whole lot of famous names. I met Mary Douglas, for example, who at dinner one evening was kind enough to point out to me who everyone else was.

Diego Maria Malara

That same year, 1973, saw the publication of Talal Asad's *Anthropology and the Colonial Encounter*. What is your perspective on colonialism and racism within social anthropology at that time?

Tim Ingold

Any thoroughgoing critique of colonialism had yet to set in. Maybe it was just beginning, but it didn't really gather steam until the late 1970s and early 80s. At that time, old colonial attitudes were still entrenched. It would be wrong to accuse anthropologists of that generation of being out-and-out racists; they were not. But they hadn't really sat down to interrogate many of the things they took for granted. An undercurrent of implicit racism was always there. For example, if someone came from Africa to do a PhD, or maybe even an undergraduate degree, and if they had a black skin, it was assumed that once they'd finished, they would go back home: they had no business in the British academic establishment. Then there was the gender bias. That was scarcely questioned at all. If you were a female anthropologist, you would be regarded as an honorary male. This happened to a string of famous women anthropologists, like Audrey Richards, Monica Wilson and Lucy Mair. Only by treating these women as men could they be accepted as 'one of us'. This attitude was still very deep-rooted at the time.

I even felt it in myself. It sometimes comes back to me with an intense sense of shame. When I was a child, my father was away a lot visiting various African countries, as he was heavily involved in setting up universities in former British colonies on the continent. But he also had a very paternalistic attitude towards Africans. He would come back and joke about the funny conversation he'd had with a native who had asked him how much he would have to pay for one of his daughters – that kind of thing. God Almighty! I was completely innocent, in a bad sense. It never even occurred to me how offensive this was, because I'd come through a thoroughly sheltered upbringing, upper-middle-class home, private education, straight to Cambridge. I had had absolutely no exposure to the rest of the world. I knew nothing about colonial history. And there was nothing in the basic anthropological training I had received to shift these attitudes. One could feel entirely comfortable. Looking back on those days, it makes me cringe with embarrassment. But then I think that, well, I've come a long way since then, and perhaps our society and system of education have too.

(C) MANCHESTER

Robert Gibb

You arrived at Manchester University in 1974. Had you applied for other jobs prior to that?

Tim Ingold

Yes, I had. There had been a possible job at University College London. Just the year before that, I was awarded a scholarship from the Finnish government to allow me to spend a year writing up in Helsinki, but at the same time as I was applying for this, I was also looking for other jobs. I remember applying for one in Birmingham, but it never came to anything, while Cambridge refused even to cover travel costs to the interview. Eventually, I had a choice between Manchester and UCL. There was no shortage of positions – quite the reverse of the situation today. But I made it only just in time. There were contemporaries of mine who opted for postdoctoral positions that would give them the chance to do more fieldwork and to spend more time on research and writing. They would get fellowships for one, two or three years, but by the time they came back on the job market for lectureships, a few years later, there was nothing left. They ended up having to leave the academy and go into development work, or something similar. We lost quite a few people that way. I was lucky to sneak in just in time. This was the period of the big cuts to universities imposed by the Thatcher government. After that there were no jobs for a decade, and a lot of redundancies as well.

Robert Gibb

When you started in Manchester, what did you find? What was the Department like?

Tim Ingold

It was a vipers' nest! I arrived in the dying days of the so-called Manchester School, and its great leader was Max Gluckman. By then he had retired and was going around the world giving lectures and being famous. He died a year after I arrived, so I met him maybe only once or twice. He never got my name right. He always called me Tom. I ended up having to play my cello at his memorial event, in front of my external examiner-to-be. It was terrifying.

The Head of Department was Emrys Peters, who had spent much of his professional life in the shadow of Gluckman. There were others from that era: Richard Werbner, Paul Baxter, Martin Southwold. I had replaced another of them, Basil Sansom, who had just left to go to Australia. And then there were more recent arrivals, including Keith Hart, David Turton and John Comaroff; they had all come a few years before me. Chris Fuller arrived at the same time as I did. There was thus a mixture of old Manchester School types and new arrivals. I just walked right into it. Emrys was a very divisive figure who loved to play people off against one another. I think he wrote two articles in his lifetime. They were both very good articles, but that was the sum total of his production. I think his behaviour, and his inability to publish, must have been partly in reaction to years of intimidation under Gluckman. He once joked that one day, he would publish his collected book contracts! But he never did.

When I arrived, they were looking for somebody to supervise the PhD research of Pnina Werbner, Dick Werbner's wife. Pnina would go on to become a very distinguished anthropologist in her own right, but at the time she was only just starting out on her research career.[2] Her research was on the Pakistani community in Manchester. Who on earth, they asked, could supervise this research? 'Ah, Tim! He's done research on an ethnic minority.' Because I'd worked with Sámi reindeer herders, they thought, I would be just the right person to supervise research on Pakistanis in Manchester. They're both ethnic minorities, after all! That's how I ended up as Pnina's supervisor. She was my very first doctoral student. In practice this was fine, because she was already a very competent researcher and knew exactly what she was doing. But I was of no help to her at

---

2 Pnina Werbner passed away in 2023. An obituary was published in *The Guardian* newspaper: https://www.theguardian.com/science/2023/mar/29/pnina-werbner-obituary.

all. What I didn't know at that time, however, was that Emrys Peters and Pnina's husband, Dick Werbner, were scarcely on speaking terms, and that Pnina was the niece of Max Gluckman! There were all these personal and kinship-related issues going on in the Department, which I blindly walked into and then had to figure out. It was hardly a harmonious environment, but it could be stimulating. There was a tradition in the Manchester School that seminars should be abrasive. The departmental seminar had this reputation: an invited speaker would turn up, give their paper and be basically torn to pieces. Stories would be told of great occasions when this or that anthropologist had been entirely dismembered. There was still a bit of this left – it took a while to go altogether – and it was strange to find myself in the middle of it all.

I was often made to feel ashamed of my fieldwork. My more senior colleagues in the Department – those remaining from the Gluckman era – couldn't understand that I had been working in Lapland, and not somewhere in Africa or the Middle East. They thought I had got pastoralism all wrong because they understood pastoralism to be what people in Africa do with cattle, or what people in the Middle East do with sheep and goats. They were quite unwilling to accept that northern pastoralists might do things differently with reindeer. You'd get these jibes like 'Are you the anthropologist with the antlers on?' or 'Did you meet Father Christmas?' Yes, it was sometimes as bad as that! As a rather insecure neophyte trying to find his feet there were times when I was made to feel that because I hadn't been working in Africa, the Middle East or South Asia, I hadn't done proper fieldwork at all – that what I had done was worthless, or good only for poking fun at. It was pretty difficult; not a healthy or supportive atmosphere at all.

But in other ways Manchester was great. I had some good colleagues among the more recent arrivals: Keith Hart, David Turton, John Comaroff, Chris Fuller. When I first arrived only one or two members of staff had telephones in their offices; it was a mark of high status. John Comaroff's office was on the other side of the corridor from mine. He had a telephone, and he would have his door open and be sitting there with his feet up on the desk and his telephone in his hand, like some newspaper proprietor, talking at great speed and using long and complicated words like 'ontology' and 'epistemology' that I'd never heard before. It was all very intimidating. I thought: 'I don't understand what's going on, and I don't have a telephone.' Then the following year, Marshall Sahlins came to visit. John made a thing of chatting up Marshall, and the next thing you know, he was off to take up a new position in Chicago. So that was that. John was a convivial colleague, but I could only ever understand half of what he was talking about.

Robert Gibb

Were there any women within the Department as colleagues?

Tim Ingold

Sue Benson came for a couple of years as a temporary lecturer. But it was a very all-male place, and the way they behaved towards Sue was appalling. It was basically a men's club; horrible. All that would later change – and change dramatically – but that's how it was when I first arrived. Moreover, in meetings and seminars you had to sit in rooms thick with smoke. Everyone smoked a pipe or very smoky cigarettes. Having never smoked myself, I would leave meetings coughing and spluttering, and with my eyes watering.

Robert Gibb

What teaching did you do in the first years? Was there a big undergraduate programme? Did you have other PhD students apart from Pnina?

Tim Ingold

I gradually acquired more doctoral students. Though Pnina was the first to start, she was not the first to finish because her research was interrupted by a period of maternity leave. My next student – in fact, the first to finish – was Gísli Pálsson. He, too, has gone on to have a very distinguished anthropological career. Gísli and I have been good friends and close colleagues ever since. But in those days, you just had to accept what PhD students you could. It had little to do with common interests; it was just a case of someone needing a supervisor.

The teaching I was first given to do was a course called 'Environment and Technology'. It was, in effect, a course in cultural ecology, and had been initiated by my predecessor, Basil Sansom, whom I had replaced following his departure to Australia. I was basically ordered to teach the course, so I did what I was told, which is perhaps the main reason why I got into ecological anthropology. I didn't know much about the subject, but teaching the course forced me to read up on it. 'Environment and Technology' was abbreviated to ET, so when the Spielberg film came out, it was nicknamed the Extra-Terrestrial. The course was indeed considered a bit alien by my colleagues in the Department, but I very much enjoyed teaching it.

Apart from that, I did stints of teaching one part of the first-year introductory course. I also taught a second-year course called 'Culture and Society', charting the history of anthropological thought along an axis from Durkheim to Mauss to Lévi-Strauss. In the third year, I alternated 'Environment and Technology' with a course in 'Anthropological Theory'. Then, when Keith Hart – who had been teaching economic anthropology – left to take up a position at Yale, I picked it up, converting 'Environment and Technology' into 'Environment and Economy'. That way, students would get a bit of both.

This all happened over the first ten years or so. I had always wanted to teach a course on the circumpolar North, but they said I couldn't teach a course on a region where no-one lived and for which there was no literature! I recall that when I was in Lapland in 1979–80, doing a second 12-month stint of fieldwork, I received a letter from Emrys, my Head of Department, instructing me that on my return, I was to teach a course on Central Africa. This region was considered sacrosanct in the Department, since it was the original cradle of the Manchester School. But I thought: 'This is ridiculous. Why should I be teaching a course on a region where I have never been and which I know nothing about?' Well, I managed to get out of it. But at the time, it was assumed that some regions of the world exist anthropologically, and others don't, and the region in which I was working definitely did not. Finally, in 1984, Emrys Peters retired. He was already ill with lung cancer thanks to having been smoking like a chimney, all day every day, and he eventually passed away in 1987. Following his retirement there was a brief interregnum, and then Marilyn Strathern arrived, in 1985. She brought in new people, and of course everything changed.

Philip Tonner

Tell us about your work at that time.

Tim Ingold

In 1986, I brought out two books. One was called *Evolution and Social Life*, a heavy-duty theoretical inquiry into how the idea of evolution has been developed and applied in the fields of history, biology and anthropology, from the mid-nineteenth century to the present. The other was called *The Appropriation of Nature: Essays on Human Ecology and Social Relations*. This latter book was largely based on my teaching for the course on environment and technology. What I'd been trying to do, and the way I had set it out in the course, was to bring together what I saw as two dimensions of human being: as a social being or person, positioned in a network of relations with other persons, and as an organism, bound with other organisms into what ecologists call a web of life. If social anthropology studies the first dimension, ecology studies the second. The question for me was: how can they be combined?

I was much influenced at the time by the work of scholars like Maurice Godelier and Emmanuel Terray, pioneers of the new school of anthropological neo-Marxism. Godelier, in particular, was attempting to show how the problem could be addressed within a Marxian analytic framework. His idea was to substitute the dichotomy between ecological and social relations for the classic Marxian division between forces and relations of production. One could then attempt to understand the interplay between the ecological and the social in some sort of dialectical fashion. I was trying to show how you could apply this model to thinking about hunter-gatherers and pastoralists, and I was keen to work on it. So that was one side of what I was doing, trying to combine ecology and social anthropology, and it was my principal theme in *The Appropriation of Nature*. On the other, evolutionary, side, I was trying to figure out how we can reconcile what we know from anthropology about people and history and relationships, with what we know from biology about human evolution. I thought it ought to be possible to put them together, somehow. *Evolution and Social Life* was my attempt to do so. It was a long book, however, and as tough going to write as it would be to read.

Both books ended in failure. With *The Appropriation of Nature*, I finally had to admit to myself that I could not carry on with this dichotomous model of the human being as one part organism, one part person; it just doesn't make sense. In writing about evolution, I had discovered the philosophical works of Henri Bergson and Alfred North Whitehead, and this had pointed me towards a third way, beyond the dichotomies of ecology and society, biology and culture, evolution and history. But to develop this third way would require a complete rewriting of biology. I couldn't carry on with the standard Darwinian or neo-Darwinian model. There followed a decade of work, closely linked to my teaching in 'Environment and Economy', trying to figure out how to reconcile social anthropology, human ecology and evolutionary biology, and finding that the only way forward is with a different ecology and a different biology. That was mostly what I was working on.

Whilst all this was happening, the Department in Manchester was going through the floor. Student recruitment fell to almost zero. There were some pretty disastrous years, from the late 1970s to the early 1980s. Emrys Peters was not well. The Department didn't have effective leadership. Nobody was interested. There was no proper PhD programme. There were a handful of doctoral students knocking around, but nothing like a programme, no recruitment. At the same time, new degree programmes were being established in subjects like Accounting and Law, which were pulling in huge numbers of students. We found ourselves in the same Faculty, of Economic and Social Studies, as the newly formed Department of Accounting and Business Finance. Of the quota of students admitted to the Faculty, most were going to Accounting, and we were left with the dregs. Numbers literally plummeted.

The great advantage of this, for me, was that with so few students, I hardly had any teaching to do. Instead, I holed myself up and got on with writing my big book on evolution. There wasn't much else to do, and nobody else in the Department was remotely interested. So I had peace and quiet to get on with it. It was just lucky for me that this low point for the Department came at the very moment when I wanted to get on with some serious writing.

I was looking for a way to reconcile social anthropology with evolutionary biology. Those were the days of the great sociobiology debate. In 1975, Edward O. Wilson had published his big textbook on the subject, *Sociobiology: The New Synthesis*, and it went on to have a massive popular impact. Everyone was going on about it. Among my social anthropological colleagues, however, it was assumed that anyone who even talked about evolution must be either some sort of relic from the Victorian era or a sociobiologist and therefore a rabid genetic determinist. You had to be one or the other. My fellow social anthropologists, both in the Department and beyond, were avidly hostile to evolutionary thinking and wanted nothing to do with it. As a result, I was largely left on my own.

When my book, *Evolution and Social Life*, eventually came out, it sank like a lump of lead. In social anthropology, the book was largely ignored. The whole topic of evolution remained pretty much taboo. But it fared no better in biology. Darwinism, at that time, was tantamount to a creed, which no-one in their right mind would presume to question. To any biologists who even looked at the book it was obvious that having done just that, I had either completely lost my mind or didn't know what I was talking about. Why else would I refer to such utterly discredited philosophers as Alfred North Whitehead and Henri Bergson? The few reviews were contemptuously dismissive. Thus the book, which I had meant to be my masterpiece, fell between the two stools of anthropology and biology, and never took off. It was a disaster. But I suppose I had to go through all this in order to find an alternative path. It is a path I discovered in the late 1980s, and I spent the 1990s following it.

Philip Tonner

At a certain point in your career, you became more attracted to phenomenology. Can you tell us why and what were the consequences of this?

Tim Ingold

Yes, it came rather belatedly. It was never my intention to become a phenomenologist. The initial influence was not phenomenology; it was James Gibson's ecological psychology, to which I was introduced almost by accident by one of its leading exponents, Edward Reed, who sadly passed away far too soon, in 1997. Ed happened to have read something I'd written; I think it was my essay – which began life as the 1982 Malinowski Memorial Lecture, and was published the following year – 'The Architect and the Bee: Reflections on the Work of Animals and Men'. In a letter, he told me that he had read this article of mine and that I really ought to read the work of James Gibson – that I would find it helpful in my effort to reconnect ecology and anthropology. Eventually I read it, and it did indeed help. More than that, I realised that in this work, which was about the possibility of a perception that is direct rather than mediated by signs and symbols, potentially lay the key to solving the problem of how to rethink human-environment relationships.

I thus began to think about how we could bring this Gibsonian idea of direct perception into anthropology. Could we see ideas, usually called 'cultural', as having their generative source in the immediate perceptual engagement of living, attentive beings, whether human or animal, with their environment? Yet despite my enthusiasm for Gibson's approach, it seemed to me rather one-sided. For while the perceiver is pictured as actively moving around in and exploring the environment, the environment itself is treated as if it consisted only of objects to be perceived. It's just there, and then the perceiver walks around in it, like an actor on a stage set. But what if the environment is just as active, just as dynamic, as the perceiver?

With this question in mind, I reached out to the work of Martin Heidegger first, and only then to Maurice Merleau-Ponty. Heidegger came first because I happened to have met an architect who told me I really had to read his essay of 1954, 'Building Dwelling Thinking'. On first reading, I couldn't understand it at all. But I nevertheless felt there was something there, and I liked the idea of dwelling. But it was Merleau-Ponty, in his magisterial *Phenomenology of Perception*, who provided the key to understanding what it means to perceive in an environment that has not yet precipitated out into the objective forms of this or that. It was in his understanding of perception as pre-objective that Merleau-Ponty takes us beyond Gibson, despite the many things their approaches have in common. And this gave me the tools I needed.

Thus, I got into phenomenology because it offered a possible way forward for where I wanted to go, not because I wanted to study phenomenology for its own sake, or wanted to become a phenomenologist. I wasn't interested in that. But among philosophers, Merleau-Ponty is remarkable for his genuine interest in empirical studies of perception; I liked that. He isn't holed up, like so many of his profession, in a philosophical bubble.

Diego Maria Malara

I have a follow-up question on the Manchester Department. You mentioned that when Marilyn Strathern came many things changed, and I wonder if you could elaborate on what these changes were. At a time when there were still few women in the Department, did the new foregrounding of gender relations create tensions?

Tim Ingold

Some would talk mockingly about our 'great leader' when Marilyn arrived. I might even have done so myself! In the first few years she was hard at work on the book that would become *The Gender of the Gift*, but she also brought along her interests in kinship and reproductive technology, which were further strengthened with the appointment of Janet Carsten in 1989. And, of course, there was her regional interest in Melanesia, which was new to the Department, and reinforced with the arrival of Jimmy Weiner, in 1990.[3] Marilyn and Jimmy were both speaking an anthropological language that owed a great deal to the writings of Roy Wagner, and which many of us – and I'll put my hand up here, because I am as guilty of this as anyone – found next to incomprehensible. So, there may have been a certain scepticism. Whether this had a gender dimension I cannot say, but it might have done. Maybe 'we' men, who had been

---

3   James Weiner, alias Jamie Pearl Bloom, sadly passed away in 2020. An obituary by Francesca Merlan and Alan Rumsey, published in *The Asia Pacific Journal of Anthropology*, can be accessed at https://www.tandfonline.com/doi/pdf/10.1080/14442213.2020.1831229.

around in Manchester for quite a few years, thought we knew how to write clearly and how to explain things. And then along comes this woman who's talking stuff we don't understand, and who doesn't have much experience of teaching or running a programme . . .

There were certainly strains between Marilyn and myself, which increased in the years running up to her departure, in 1993, to take up the William Wyse Professorship in Social Anthropology at Cambridge. In those years I was editing the journal *Man* from a tiny cupboard of an office, affectionately known as 'the manhole', at the far end of the Departmental corridor, while she occupied the professorial suite halfway down, and this continued even for a few months after I had taken over from her as Head of Department. To put it as diplomatically as I can, I don't think there was room for both of us on the same corridor. I felt more comfortable once I could run things my way. I was Head of Department from 1993 to 1997. During that time the Department's fortunes were on the rise again, with many new appointments and a flourishing doctoral programme. And as for the journal, although I had by then completed my stint as editor, I had at last managed to get its name changed. Can you imagine a journal entitled *Man*, in which the 'instructions for authors' recommend the use of gender-neutral language at all times? From 1994, it reverted to its historic title, *Journal of the Royal Anthropological Institute*. Future editors would no longer receive invitations, as I did, to sumptuous gentlemen's fashion events.

(D) ABERDEEN

Diego Maria Malara

In 1999 you were appointed to a Chair in Social Anthropology at the University of Aberdeen, and you had also been invited to set up a new department there, which was established in 2002. This is not something one is asked to do every day. What was it like to do such a thing? What was your vision at the time, and what were the challenges?

Tim Ingold

No, it isn't something one is asked to do every day. One of the things that attracted me was the chance to make a fresh start. The alternative would have been to stay in Manchester for the rest of my days, getting in the way of a younger generation wanting to make their mark. I was invited to set up a new anthropology programme at Aberdeen, initially within the framework of the Department of Sociology. Apart from a brief stint in Helsinki in 1973-4, I had never worked in a sociology department before, or had sociologists as colleagues, so this was a new and challenging experience in itself. But anthropology had previously been taught in the Sociology Department, back in the early 1980s, before it fell victim to the Thatcher government's cuts. Three of the four anthropologists on the staff at that time were redeployed to other institutions and the fourth, Mark Nuttall, stayed in place as a member of staff of the Sociology Department. They weren't therefore completely new to anthropology. Nevertheless, most of the sociologists had a picture of anthropology dating from something like the mid-1960s. It was a view of anthropology that I scarcely recognised, and which I only vaguely remembered from my student days.

Strictly speaking, I had not been invited to set up a department. But it was always my intention to do so. And it was bound to be subversive, at least in the eyes of my new colleagues in Sociology. The question was: how to go about it? How, starting virtually from scratch, was I to begin setting up a proper anthropological outfit, a real department? At that time, the university was small, a bit chaotic, but very dynamic. It had gone through a bad patch in the 1980s. By the early 1990s, however, it had a new Principal, Duncan Rice. Duncan was a historian and an intellectual who loved big ideas. There was a real sense that you could do things. But the administration was so chaotic that nobody could tell me exactly what I was supposed to do. I could just get on with it, and do what I wanted.

I began by looking around the University for anyone with anthropological interests. And I found a few, in two places in particular. There was a programme in cultural history which was based in the History Department but actually led by an anthropologist, Elizabeth Hallam, and there was also the so-called Elphinstone Institute, which specialises in the people and culture of northeast Scotland. The Institute functioned, in effect, as a department of regional ethnology. Under its previous leadership it had become somewhat moribund, but a new director, Ian Russell, had just been appointed, and was seeking to revive its fortunes. So the first thing to do, I thought, would be to set up a seminar that would bring together all these colleagues from cultural history and the Elphinstone Institute, along with anyone else with similar concerns, to talk among ourselves about shared interests. Then, once we had got used to meeting together, we would start inviting outside speakers. The seminar came to be known as SAnECH, an acronym for 'social anthropology, ethnology and cultural history'. This, then, served as the foundation stone for our programme.

I took my model for building a department from my earlier fieldwork with small farmers in Lapland. If you are a farmer, and you're creating a new farm out of the wilderness of forest and swamp, the first thing to do is build a sauna. You and your family live in the sauna while you build the cowshed. And once you have a place for your cows, then you can build your dwelling house, move in and start living there. So that was the model I adopted.

The seminar was the sauna. You start with a seminar, get a bunch of people with anthropological interests together, get them talking. Thus, we had our seminar, which was meeting every week. My sociological colleagues were very worried about this: 'What's he up to?' they would whisper in corridors. 'He was supposed to be with us, but now he is sleeping with all these other people.' They weren't too happy about the SAnECH seminar, but it was very successful. Then, we used the seminar as the basis to establish a postgraduate programme, which meant going through a lot of bureaucratic hoops to get ourselves 'kitemarked' by the Economic and Social Research Council. The programme was officially recognised in 2000. With that, the cowshed was in place. Then, all we had to do was build our department, the dwelling house. We were able to establish a new department in 2002 because, at that time, the university abolished Faculties and set up a structure of Schools in its place. We had been in the Faculty of Economic and Social Studies, as I think it was called. But with the establishment of the new School of Social Science, we had the opportunity to join with the Departments of Sociology and Politics & International Relations (PIR) as a separate Department of Anthropology. It was a trick of a sort, but we got away with it. Nevertheless, Departments weren't officially recognised in the School model. They existed only *de facto*, so all we needed to get our own Department established in 2002 was to have the University printer supply us with headed notepaper with 'Department of Anthropology' proudly displayed at the top of the page! With that, we had a department.

Our undergraduate programme started with its first year in October 1999. Thus, the first students, following the four years of the Scottish degree, graduated in 2003. Though we gradually built on this, my view from the start was that the way to grow the Department was through the development of its postgraduate programme: we had to recruit Masters and PhD students, particularly the latter. If the graduate programme is functioning well, and bringing students in, then, I believed, the undergraduate programme would take care of itself. One of the reasons why it was so important for us to have our own Department was that the Sociology Department was following the opposite strategy under its then head, Steve Bruce. Steve was trying to put as many 'bums on seats' as possible, and that meant the mass teaching of undergraduates: 'That will ensure our numbers are sound,' he explained, 'so we get the resources we need.' And it worked for him, because there were lots of students wanting to read sociology. But he couldn't care less about graduate students. 'Who on earth would want to come to Aberdeen to do a PhD in sociology?' he once said to me, 'maybe the odd oil-wife.'

Aberdeen, of course, is one of the world's leading centres for the oil and gas industry, on which the city's prosperity largely depends. Perhaps the wife of an oil-rig worker, having nothing better to do with her time, might fancy studying for a higher degree in sociology? That was what Steve thought. But I was convinced that if we were going to succeed in building up an anthropology department, then we would have to focus our energy on doctoral students. Within the space of a decade, we already had 35 PhD students working in the Department. I recently counted up the total number of PhD students who have graduated from our Department since its foundation, and it is close to ninety! We've had two or three times as many PhD students as they've had in Sociology and PIR put together.

I also had a certain vision of anthropology in terms of where I wanted it to go. We started off with a focus on the anthropology of the North, and it worked very well for us, because it meant we could start by positioning ourselves within a network of other institutions spanning the Nordic countries, the Baltic States, Russia, Canada and Alaska. So, to the people down south who would say: 'Aberdeen? Where on earth is that? Somewhere near the North Pole, I suppose. Why have anthropology in such a remote place?' we could respond: 'You are in fact the ones who are remote; we're actually in the centre of what is an international network from the start. And by the way, much more interesting anthropology is going on in places like Copenhagen, Oslo, Tromsø, Stockholm, Helsinki, Reykjavik, Tallinn, St Petersburg, Toronto, British Columbia and Alaska than in Oxford, Cambridge and London!'

But I also wanted to bring in a set of interests around environmental perception, human–animal relations, creativity, art and architecture. From the start we had these two strands: the anthropology of the North, and what we called 'culture, creativity and perception'. We developed both in parallel. We had a very clear vision of where we were taking anthropology. It was not exactly a school of thought; rather a particular sense of what the discipline is, and where we wanted to go with it, to take it forward. As I keep saying, if you want to build a department with a reputation, it's no good simply following the trends. Rather than 'Everybody else is doing this, so we had better do the same ourselves', you have to say: 'Where do we want anthropology to be ten years from now? What are we going to do to get it there?'

When I became Head of the School of Social Science a decade later, in 2008, and found myself having to deal with colleagues in

Sociology and in PIR, I would attend departmental meetings and find them obsessed with strategies and rankings. I'd say to them: 'Well, where do you want Sociology, or PIR, to be in 10 years' time?' They had no idea. 'What do you need to do to take Sociology, or PIR, there?' Again, they hadn't thought about that. They were only interested in how to improve their rankings. It never occurred to them that they might devote a departmental meeting to discussing the future of their subject. One of the great things about our Department, which I'm very proud of, is that this is precisely what we do. Visitors to the Department always remark upon the fact that there seems to be a bunch of people here who are actually talking anthropology amongst themselves: not just about how we can keep up with the discipline, but about where we are going to take it, in the ways we want.

Diego Maria Malara

That's very interesting. No other anthropology department in the UK focuses so closely on that specific geographical area. . . .

Tim Ingold

There have been departments which, at various times in their history, have had a very strong regional focus. Remember the Manchester School and Central Africa! Here in Scotland, Edinburgh has an African Studies Centre and a very strong tradition of research in India and South Asia. St Andrews has long been specialising in Latin America. We in Aberdeen do the circumpolar North. That makes for a good complementarity of regional interests. But although we started off with the North and our research is still concentrated there, you can't build a department on one geographic region alone. There came a point when we had to diversify. So we now have staff working in Latin America, such as Maggie Bolton in Bolivia, Martin Mills in Tibet, Johan Rasanayagam in Central Asia, and so on.

Diego Maria Malara

Did the results match the plan?

Tim Ingold

Yes, on the whole. I remember it felt like climbing a mountain – and not quite knowing, for the first few years, if it was going to work out or if we would slide back down again – and then reaching some sort of plateau. Once we had consolidated undergraduate and research numbers, and staff numbers had reached 12 or 13, I really had a sense that that we'd made it. I know it sounds a bit corny, but I did have a vision of a sort, and I think we managed to realise it. But the trouble is that under current conditions, you can never say: 'Whew! We've made it to the summit. Now we can sit back and relax and enjoy the ride.' Because there's always the possibility that everything you've worked for will suddenly be wiped out. This very nearly happened to us because we had a change of leadership at the top of the University when Duncan Rice retired. We had to appoint a replacement Principal and we got Ian Diamond, whose tenure at the University was something of a disaster. He replaced what had been the laissez-faire intellectualism under Duncan Rice with a regime of intense micromanagement. Everything was about performance management, assessment, rankings. Everybody was under the screw, morale slumped, there were threats of redundancies, good people were leaving.

In 2015 we held a big international conference to celebrate the achievements of the Department.[4] But the University management had not the slightest interest in it. And it went on against the backdrop of most of our staff not knowing from one day to the next whether they still had a job. We lost a few without replacement, but we survived. Today, there's a worrying drop in undergraduate

---

4 This was the conference 'Beyond Perception 15', held in Aberdeen, 1–4 September 2015.

numbers, but I think this is happening in anthropology programmes across the board in the UK. It has so often happened in the past, in so many institutions, that everything seems to come together very nicely, only to fall apart again after a few years. This has always been the worry at the back of my mind.

Philip Tonner

Around the time you arrived at Aberdeen, your intellectual interests changed again. Can you tell us more about that change?

Tim Ingold

Throughout the 1990s, I had been trying to put together a synthesis of anthropology with phenomenology, ecological psychology and developmental biology, and all that came together in my big book of essays, *The Perception of the Environment*. I was literally doing the final tasks, like checking the proofs and whatnot, just as we were moving to Aberdeen. So that was a Manchester book, although it was published in 2000, the year after I arrived. Once I had finished it, I felt for a while that I had nothing new to say. Every time I tried to say something, I ended up merely repeating what I had said already. So I didn't mind taking time out to build a department. I could put all my energy into that, while pondering where to go next with my own research. Just at that time, moreover, new possibilities were beginning to emerge in the intersection of anthropology, art and architecture. In the years just prior to my leaving Manchester, we happened to have had a wonderful group of doctoral students with a shared background or interests in art, architecture or both. We had begun to think about how to put these fields together, and to this end, we had established what we called an 'art, architecture and anthropology' seminar. The seminar had been immensely productive, and it had been my ambition to develop it further in Aberdeen, alongside our interests in the North.

Life and career

But at some stage in all this, I also got interested in lines. In 2003 I was invited to give the Rhind Lectures, an annual series organised by the Society of Antiquaries of Scotland and held at the Royal Museums of Scotland in Edinburgh. The lectures were called 'Lines from the Past: Towards an anthropological archaeology of inscriptive practices'. They became the basis for my book *Lines: A Brief History*, first published in 2007. Several things lay behind my project on lines. One was that I had become interested in the relationship between writing and musical notation, in part through supervising the doctoral research of Kawori Iguchi. Kawori had been working on Japanese traditional music, and had learned to play the Japanese flute. She came back from the field with samples of musical notation, of a kind I had never seen before. We were working on it together. I became fascinated by how musical notation had evolved, both in Japan and in the West, and wanted to explore how it related to writing and its evolution.

At that time, I was still based in Manchester. But soon after my arrival in Aberdeen, I developed an interest in walking. This came about, above all, through working with an Aberdeen-based colleague in cultural geography, Hayden Lorimer. On Hayden's initiative, we undertook a collaborative project on ways of walking, with first Katrin Lund and subsequently Jo Lee Vergunst as the lead researcher. Hayden eventually left to take up a position in Glasgow, and is now Professor of Geography in Edinburgh. But as our walking project evolved, I was also getting interested in issues around the meaning of creativity. In 2005, the Department hosted the annual conference of the Association of Social Anthropologists on the theme 'Creativity and Cultural Improvisation', and with my colleague Elizabeth Hallam, we went on to edit an eponymous conference volume, published in 2007. So I tried to pull these three things together: lines, walking, creativity. Eventually, I began writing again, and thinking about how I could move beyond the position I had developed in *The Perception of the Environment*. This was to think more about lines, meshworks and atmospheres. All this grew into another book of essays, *Being Alive*, published in 2011.

The other thing I should mention, in closing, is that for years I had been working in the field of hunter-gatherer studies, with a strong emphasis on ecological anthropology. There had been a series of international conferences on hunting and gathering societies, going right back to one held at the London School of Economics in 1986, which I had helped to organise. The ninth conference in the series was held in Edinburgh in 2002. I co-convened the conference with my Edinburgh colleague Alan Barnard.[5] It was held on the campus of Heriot-Watt University. Though extremely stressful to organise, the conference was a great success. However, I made a conscious decision, there and then: that once it was over, I would have nothing more to do with hunter-gatherer studies. I would completely draw a line under it, because I had said everything I had to say on the subject. I couldn't contribute anything more – not, at least, without doing a whole lot more research. Instead, I wanted to pursue my new interests in lines, meshworks and atmospheres. So, to anyone who asked me to write anything on hunter-gatherer studies, or to contribute to a conference, I could respond: 'No, I'm not doing that anymore.' That was really a life-saver for me, because it left me free to develop this new field on the interface between anthropology, art and architecture. And that's what I've been doing ever since.

Further Reading

Previously published interviews with Ingold include Ergül (2017), Ferrández (2013) and Kaartinen (2018). Gibb, Malara and Tonner also interviewed Ingold in an online event organised by the Glasgow Anthropology Network (2020).

Ingold has reflected on his upbringing in a number of publications, including the Preface to the 2016 edition of *Lines* (2016a: xv–xviii)

---

5 Alan Barnard sadly passed away in 2022. An obituary, by Thomas Widlok and Akira Tahada, is published in the journal *Anthropology Today* 39(3), June 2023, page 26.

and his article 'From Science to Art and Back Again: The Pendulum of an Anthropologist' (2018c). Amongst the first books Ingold encountered in social anthropology, he mentions Barth's *Political Leadership Among Swat Pathans* (1965) and Radcliffe-Brown's *Structure and Function in Primitive Society* (1952). For general accounts of the development of British social anthropology in the twentieth century, see Kuper (2014) and Mills (2008). On the Manchester School of anthropology, see Evens and Handelman (2006).

Ingold's explorations of the relation between social and ecological systems began with his 1982 Malinowski Memorial Lecture, 'The Architect and the Bee' (Ingold 1983), and developed into his first essay collection, *The Appropriation of Nature* (Ingold 1986b). In this he was influenced by works in neo-Marxist anthropology, including Godelier's *Rationality and Irrationality in Economics* (1972) and Terray's *Marxism and 'Primitive' Societies* (1972), as well by Gibson's *The Ecological Approach to Visual Perception* (1979). His book *Evolution and Social Life* (Ingold 1986a), written in the shadow of Wilson's *Sociobiology* (1975), was strongly influenced by the philosophical works of Bergson (*Creative Evolution*, 1911) and Whitehead (*Process and Reality*, 1929). On his introduction to phenomenology, Ingold mentions Heidegger's seminal essay from 1954, Building, Dwelling, Thinking (Heidegger 2013), and Merleau-Ponty's *Phenomenology of Perception*, dating from 1945 (Merleau-Ponty 1962).

Ingold also refers to the work of Strathern (*The Gender of the Gift*, 1988) and Weiner (*The Empty Place*, 1991), both influenced by Wagner's *The Invention of Culture*, first published in 1975. A new edition of Wagner's classic, including a foreword by Ingold, was published in 2016. The Aberdeen-based walking project to which Ingold refers led to a volume co-edited with Lee Vergunst, *Ways of Walking* (Ingold and Lee Vergunst 2008), and the 2005 ASA conference to a volume co-edited with Hallam, *Creativity and Cultural Improvisation* (Hallam and Ingold 2007).

For reasons of space, Ingold's work on hunter-gatherers, which he mentions towards the end of this interview, is not explored in depth here. Interested readers are referred in particular to *Hunters, Pastoralists and Ranchers* (Ingold 1980) and *Hunters and Gatherers, Vols I: History, Evolution and Social Change*, and *II: Property, Power and Ideology* (Ingold, Riches and Woodburn 1988).

CONVERSATION 2:

Anthropology, ethnography, education and the university

> **Summary:** In this interview, Ingold considers the nature of anthropology as a discipline, the relationship between anthropology and education, and the contemporary university. He begins by outlining his views on 'theory' in anthropology, including the importance of theoretical debates and the political nature of theory. This is followed by a series of reflections on how legacies from the colonial past continue to shape anthropology and how the discipline still needs to be 'decolonised'. Ingold then summarises his understanding of the relationship between anthropology and ethnography, and reflects on the debate that his essay 'anthropology is not ethnography' has provoked. This leads on to a discussion of the relationship between anthropology and education and, finally, to an account of his involvement in the 'Reclaiming Our University' movement at the University of Aberdeen. The interview took place on 12 April 2021.

(A) ANTHROPOLOGY, THEORY AND DEBATES

Robert Gibb

In 1987 you initiated a discussion with some colleagues based in British anthropology departments that led to the creation of the

'Group for Debates in Anthropological Theory' (GDAT). In the 'Preface' to the published version of the first six debates, in the book *Key debates in anthropology*, you write that 'Debate ... is the very *modus vivendi* of theory. And theory, since it is about how we engage with the world and not just about how we represent it, is inherently political.'[1] Please could you tell us more about your views on 'theory' in anthropology, including the importance of theoretical debates and the political nature of theory.

Tim Ingold

Well, the first thing I mean is that theory is another word for thinking. I'm strongly against the idea that theories are coherent frameworks or structures, which you can pick up ready-made, and then apply to some body of data. I don't think many anthropologists would hold such a view, but it is common in other disciplines, particularly in the sciences. That's what a theory is understood to be: you should get your theory; then you should get your data; you should analyse the data by means of the theory and come up with some results; and then those results might make you want to modify the theory in this way or that. But in my understanding, theory is a process, not a structure, and as a process it carries on. It is carried on in a kind of thinking that is not private to any one individual but in some way collective, like a conversation. Theorising is something that people do together, a way of thinking together with your colleagues or students, or with the authors of the works you're reading. But it's a thinking that is inherently dialogical. With this approach there can be no real distinction between theory and practice, or between pure theory and its application; it's just theory. So that's the first thing. I wanted to stress that this is what we mean when we talk about doing theory in anthropology. We need to make this clear, particularly to students. We have to get across the point that we can't go shopping for theory as in a supermarket, picking up what we need off the shelf, ready to use. And we need

1 See Ingold (1996a: xi).

to remember, too, that theory is never finished. It is always work in progress.

Secondly, on the political dimension: the politics lies in the very fact that you are thinking *with* the world. It is a form of engagement. And for this reason, it cannot *not* be political. What is politics, after all, if not a field of public engagement? We don't have to bring in issues of power and exploitation and all that, though we could if we wanted. *Dialogical thinking in the public domain*: that basically is my understanding of what politics is. And it is also what theory is. That's why it is political.

I would like to say the same about writing. We think as we write; we write as we think. It's very hard – maybe impossible – to say where thinking ends and writing begins. If dialogical thinking in the public domain is political, then the same goes for writing. The *act* of writing is political. It makes no difference whether we write *about* politics or not; indeed, it doesn't matter what we're writing about, or thinking about, or theorising about. It's in the theorising itself, the thinking and the writing – *that's* where the politics is.

Robert Gibb

The other question I had in this section relates directly to this. A recurrent criticism of your work, including from many who are otherwise sympathetic (Alf Hornborg and Penny Howard are two recent examples), is that it pays insufficient attention to 'politics' and notably the role of political economy. In an article published in 2005, in the journal *Conservation and Society*, you reflect on precisely this point, but I was wondering if you could you tell us how you would respond to such criticism today. You've started talking about it in your first answer, but what is the place of politics and political analysis in your work?

Tim Ingold

Yes, I am often criticised for leaving politics out. Sometimes I think this is fair; sometimes not. To be honest, I feel a bit ambivalent about it. There is substance to the criticism. It's certainly true that if you were to look up almost anything I've written, apart from that one article you mention in which I address the issue head on, you would find no explicit reference to politics. If you look up the word 'politics' in the index or do a word search in any of my books, you will hardly find any instances of it. This is because I'm not really writing *about* politics, nor do I offer much by way of political analysis.

To my mind, there's a weak excuse and a strong excuse for this absence. The weak excuse is: 'Well, why should I?' I mean, as scholars we can be interested in all sorts of things. If we happen to be political analysts, then we're obviously interested in politics. But let's imagine an archaeologist interested in the manufacture of flint tools from the so-called Levalloisian period. Suppose you say to this specialist in Middle Stone Age lithic technology: 'I don't like your work; there's no mention of politics in it. Where's the political analysis?' They'd likely respond: 'Look here, that's just not what I'm working on.' I could say the same, I could say: 'Look, my interests are in perception, in skill, in the ways things are built and made. Why should this be invalidated or weakened by the fact that I don't explicitly address politics?' One could even put the boot onto the other foot, and ask of those who *do* spend their lives writing about politics whether they have even one useful thing to say about perception, or skill acquisition, or making. They don't! So why is it all right to write about politics, but not all right to write about these other themes? This, however, is a weak excuse – to say: 'Well, I can't be bothered with politics. I'm interested in other things.'

The strong excuse is one I've already hinted at. I believe my work is *intensely* political, but the politics lies in the writing, in the arguing. This writing and arguing has involved direct, hands-on struggle, in which I've faced real intimidation. I get rather annoyed with academics who pose as political analysts, occupying a comfortable, protected pulpit from which they can deliver their analyses, as if from on high, without ever having to engage with the opposition on the pitch. A lot of what I've written, for example, takes issue with cognitive science and neo-Darwinian biology. When you look at the conceptual underpinning of these fields, their funding, their institutional position, the ways they work, you see at once that they are largely feeding on the power of corporations and the state, which they in turn reinforce. By attacking them, you're attacking the very political structure on which these paradigms rest, or on which they thrive. And yet neo-Darwinian biology and cognitive science present themselves as if they were entirely *apolitical*, as purely scientific. But we know very well that they're not. We know that they rest on structures of power. For example, the way in which neo-Darwinists rank scientists like themselves, who claim to reason from evidence, over tribespeople alleged to be mere puppets of their genetically or culturally inherited traits, is manifestly colonial! But scientists are unaware of this presumption of superiority, and never address it. Engaging with their arguments, calling out the biases they contain, is not just political, it is viscerally so. You feel it in the brickbats you get from those who consider themselves to be beyond critique, especially if it comes from an anthropologist. I've been there; it's tough and you have to be pretty thick-skinned to survive. That's where the politics is.

There's one other way in which I think we should understand our own writing as political, and that is in how we address our readers. So much academic writing is deliberately exclusionary. It's exclusionary in that it assumes on the part of readers a knowledge of a certain body of literature, which the author happens to be vested in, and a facility in using often quite arcane concepts. You have to be able to talk the talk. One of the worst offenders in this regard is postcolonial theory. Theorists of this persuasion couch their arguments in a deliberately obfuscating language that only other academics working in their field can be expected to understand. What this does is reproduce the very structures of academic power that they claim to be deconstructing, and which themselves have a colonial foundation. I find that downright hypocritical!

Diego Maria Malara

I have a couple of very quick follow-ups, Tim. First of all: would it be correct to say that underpinning your complex explanation or justification is actually a significantly different vision of politics?

Tim Ingold

It could be, yes. It's certainly a different vision, I think, of democratic politics. Democracy is one of those words that can be understood in a million ways and, as you know, some pretty atrocious things have been justified in its name. It's not a good in itself unless we can explain what we mean by it. We'll come later to the writings of John Dewey but, for me, in recent years, they have been inspirational, particularly in his understanding of democracy as a way of *living together in difference* – as a way in which we engage unceasingly in conversation with others, and in which common ground is something we work collectively to co-create rather than a necessary and assumed point of departure. That's not majoritarian; it has nothing to do with who gets the most votes. It has to do with the quality and nuance of public discourse.

I feel that in many spheres of our society, nowadays, politics is being cheapened. You know how sociologists go on about intersectionality? There's race, power, gender, class, ethnicity and maybe a few other things – and that's it. For them, politics lies in the way these intersect. This idea, that individual selfhood is effectively determined by the intersection of a bunch of sociological categories, is so reductionist! It takes the atomisation of hyper-modernism to a new level. I find it deeply dehumanising – insensitive to difference, to the variations of human experience which can so enrich democratic conversations. There's such a negative, even cynical, tone to it. So, I think, yes, if we go back to the idea of politics as dialogue, as conversation, of living with difference in the public domain, then it would be a different definition from the kind that starts directly from the power relations of class, race, gender and exploitation.

Diego Maria Malara

Thanks. You say that theory for you is not just about representing the world; it's about how we engage with it. What does this statement about engaging with the world rather than representing it concretely mean? I was wondering if you were responding to the kind of debates associated with *Writing Culture* (Clifford and Marcus 1986)?

Tim Ingold

Not really, no. I have to confess that I find all these debates around the crisis of representation, which students are still expected to wade through, unbearably tedious. I have tried to keep them at arm's length. I didn't want to bother with them. I'm not sure why. Partly I just felt that it was very inward-looking – a case of anthropologists looking at their own navels. Obviously, there was cause for it. There is no doubt that we were transiting from the old days of structural functionalism, when you would go out to the field, collect your material, do your analysis, and write it up as an authoritative account of how the society in question functions. Clearly, we had reached a stage in anthropology where this no longer worked; structural functionalism was collapsing along with the colonial apparatus on which it rested. We were in a state of flux, and unsure where to go instead. The crisis of representation was part of this.

But I found the whole way the debate was conducted terribly introverted. There was no real interest in engaging with the thinking of other disciplines. To my mind, it was largely responsible for turning anthropology into the study of itself. A student contemplating going to study anthropology at university might be thinking: 'This looks like a great subject. I want to learn about my fellow human beings, what they do, how they live.' And so they go to university with their head full of hopes and dreams about anthropology and what it's going to give them. And what do they get? Angst-ridden explanations of how to do (or not to do) anthropology. They find anthropologists apparently uninterested in other human beings, worrying only about themselves. This is to get our priorities back to front: as though people existed for the purpose of writing anthropology, rather than anthropology for the purpose of understanding people. While all this *Writing Culture* thing was going on, I was still with Marx. I was thinking: 'Here's a world. What's it like? How can we change it?'

(B) ANTHROPOLOGY, POLITICS AND THE COLONIAL LEGACY

Robert Gibb

In an 'Afterword' to a recent edited collection discussing your work, Tim, you write: 'My purpose is . . . to demolish the walls that divide the land of academia from the rest of the world, and to expose the conceit of its inhabitants – a conceit that lingers as an uncomfortable legacy from the colonial past – that they alone are equipped to tackle questions of so deep a nature as to elude ordinary folk. Are humans not all students of social life by the very fact of living it?'[2] Please could you tell us more about this: the nature of this aim, how it might be achieved and what some of the key obstacles are that will need to be overcome.

Tim Ingold

This anticipates the questions about anthropology and ethnography that we're going to come to later, because I think one of the major obstacles lies in the structure of the academy. I believe the professionalisation of anthropology, in the practice of ethnography, upholds that structure.

---

2 See Ingold (2021a: 143).

Maybe by comparing ourselves with another discipline, say psychology, we can see more clearly where the problem lies. If you were a psychologist, you would consider your discipline to be one that studies people – or 'carries out research among human subjects', as research funders like to put it. Anthropologists would say the same. So, what's the difference? You might answer that psychologists are interested in the mind, whereas anthropologists are interested in society. But that doesn't get us very far. If you were to ask them, most psychologists would explain that theirs is primarily an experimental discipline, and that what it tries to do is find out about human minds, how they work, what's inside them. So the people with whom, or rather *on* whom, the psychologist works are a resource from which to extract data. The researcher might, for example, be carrying out attitude surveys, finding out what attitudes people hold and how they influence behaviour. But whatever the specific topic of inquiry, they are treating the people as repositories from which to extract information, whether through conducting experiments or administering questionnaires. They will then analyse the data in order to come up with pronouncements about how minds work, or how their owners behave. What they're *not* doing is listening to what the people themselves have to say, for its own sake, or engaging in any kind of conversation with them.

The best thing about anthropology, it seems to me, is that regardless of what subsequently happens with their material, as least during fieldwork anthropologists are actually listening to people, interested in what they have to say and anxious to learn from it. Most anthropologists today would acknowledge that the people with whom they work are every bit their equal. They're just as intelligent, their ideas are worth as much. When we speak together, it's a conversation, a dialogue; it's not *us* researching *them*. Most anthropologists would accept this. But when you look around at other disciplines, anthropology does indeed appear unique in this regard. What other discipline is doing this, having serious conversations with the people with whom they study? I don't think this is true of any other discipline. But the trouble is that as soon as we present the conversations we've been having, and the ideas that emerge from them, as *ethnography*, then it is immediately back to 'us' versus 'them' again, the researcher versus the researched.

Suppose that, as an educator, you are having conversations in the classroom with your students. Would you say you were making an ethnographic study of them? Of course not! Nor would anyone suppose, when the students are listening to their professor, that their purpose is to collect the ethnographic material they would need to write the professor up. Clearly, then, ethnography is understood as something to be done *outside* the academy. Anthropology, by contrast, is what you do with students and colleagues *inside* it. My big worry is that in rendering what we do outside the academy as ethnography, and inside it as anthropology, we are actually complicit in protecting and reinforcing this barrier between the academy and the rest of the world. In my view, the mission of anthropology is to break this barrier down! I want to insist that we are doing anthropology wherever we are, as much in conversations with people beyond the academy as with students and colleagues within it. And this is the point at which we can begin to think of anthropology as primarily educational rather than ethnographic – in a specific sense of education that we'll come to later.

When all is said and done, however, this logic – which turns accounts of others, or of our engagements with them, into ethnography – is merely a local anthropological manifestation of a much more general move by which the academy preserves its authority as a place dedicated to producing superior knowledge of how the world works, destined to be disseminated to the supposedly ignorant masses. This is a colonial legacy, or a legacy of the Enlightenment, or actually both, seeing as the Enlightenment and colonialism have always been joined at the hip.

Robert Gibb

Just to follow on from that: as you know, there's currently (and there has been before as well, it's not entirely new) a debate on how anthropology, and other disciplines, could be decolonised. What other legacies from the colonial past, apart from the one you've just been discussing, do you think continue to shape contemporary anthropology? In what ways do you think anthropology still needs to be 'decolonised'?

Tim Ingold

I don't know if you're seeing the same thing in your Department, but in ours in Aberdeen, students are now actively debating the whole issue of decolonisation. The debate is long overdue. Since I'm now retired, I've been watching it from the sidelines. It's been interesting. I recently read the report of a student group from another Department (not ours); they brought up a point with which I absolutely agree, concerning the notion of cultural diversity. That is: there's a distinction to be made between diversity and difference. As soon as we render difference as diversity, we position ourselves as standing above all the variation, boxing it up into varieties, so that everyone in each box is the same in being of this variety or that, and exporting all difference onto the dividing lines between them. This is definitely a colonial move.

One thing I think we urgently need to do is to expunge the idea of cultural diversity from the anthropological curriculum, and insert difference in its place, while making it quite clear how and why the two concepts are not the same. I mean, difference is ongoing differentiation; it's about the way in which we continually forge our own sense of who we are in and through our relations with others. It's about *becoming* different. That's where all the creativity of social life is to be found, and it is where anthropology comes into its element. But as soon as we render this as diversity, we've got it all wrapped up. Difference becomes division, between one social or cultural category and another. It is quite a challenge to liberate anthropology, and particularly the teaching of anthropology, from this sort of mentality. I think it's the biggest task of decolonising we have – bigger than all these intersecting categorisations of race, gender and so on. Or rather, it subsumes all of them.

Diego Maria Malara

I'm not entirely sure I understand: what is diversity for you then, and how do you concretely go about liberating teaching from this kind of emphasis?

Tim Ingold

Well, diversity, to my ear, implies difference that has precipitated out, as it were, from the flow of social life, and is already partitioned into categories. With this, difference gives way to division, to the logic of 'us' and 'them', according to which I belong to this group because I'm not of that group. It is based on the presumption that the world of human relations, or indeed of relations among living creatures of any kind, is primordially divided. It is classificatory. This of course was long built into the assumptions of mainstream social anthropology. When I was an undergraduate in Cambridge in the late 1960s, and we were all reading Edmund Leach, that's exactly what he said: it's just the way the world is, divided into in-groups and out-groups, and we have to start from there. As Leach put it in his BBC Reith Lectures of 1967, all difference is contrastive: '*I* identify myself with a collective *we*, which is then contrasted with some *other*.'[3] This is nonsense. We know very well that the world isn't sliced up like that. But that's what was assumed at the time.

It might help to compare the way anthropologists talk about cultural diversity with the way biologists talk about *bio*diversity. By that, they usually mean an environment with room for lots of different species. But they're already assuming they can map out, from a superior vantage point, what all these different species are. Every species is like an entry in a catalogue, compiled by science. But scientists themselves aren't in the catalogue! Nor are anthropologists in their catalogue of culture. If you were an ant in the rainforest, you

---

3   These lectures were subsequently published under the title *A Runaway World?* (Leach 1967). The quotation is from page 34.

probably wouldn't see the rainforest in terms of biodiversity; you would see it in terms of what you have to do to live as an ant! You wouldn't see all these different types, because you would not have a bird's eye view of the whole thing. It's the same with people.

Diego Maria Malara

Your interest, then, is on the emergent nature of concepts and categories and how they are made and unmade?

Tim Ingold

Yes, that's right.

(C) ANTHROPOLOGY, ETHNOGRAPHY AND PARTICIPANT OBSERVATION

Robert Gibb

We've already started talking about this a bit, so let's move on to anthropology, ethnography and participant observation. As we've already discussed in relation to the Group for Debates in Anthropology, you view debate as central to theory and, more generally, to the intellectual vitality of disciplines such as anthropology. Through a series of articles from your 2007 Radcliffe-Brown Lecture onwards, you have initiated and helped to develop an important debate about anthropology and ethnography. As you've already intimated, your understanding of the relationship between anthropology and ethnography seems to differ from conventional understandings within the discipline, and you also take issue with the conflation of ethnography and fieldwork. Could you explain here what you mean by these terms and why you see the need to reformulate the relation between them?

Tim Ingold

Let's start with ethnography and fieldwork. The thing is that what we call fieldwork is simply a period of time you spend as a researcher with a bunch of people somewhere, in whose lives you are interested, for whatever reason. You do your participant observation, you write your diary every day, you do all these things you should do. It's conventional in the discipline to describe this person, who is doing their fieldwork and writing their fieldnotes, as an 'ethnographer'. I feel this is wrong, or at least that it brings in presumptions which are ethically problematic. It comes, for example, when we refer to 'the ethnographic encounter'. I mean, in ordinary life – forget about anthropology, just in ordinary life – you encounter people all the time. When you bump into a friend in the supermarket and stop to chat, you wouldn't call it an ethnographic encounter. It's just an encounter. You might learn things from your chat; you might even write about them in your diary. You might reflect on what you've heard, or tell your friends about it, or in your letters to them. So, all this is going on. And my feeling is that, well, that's also what goes on in the course of fieldwork: that there's only one difference between fieldwork and ordinary life, namely, that you are likely to be more systematic about remembering what people have told you, and more insistent in asking questions. You might be a bit like a detective – someone who has really got their ear to the ground and is following every possible clue in order to uncover the plot, rather than listening with only half an ear, as we commonly do in everyday life, while thinking about something else. A good fieldworker is a person who is ever attentive, who really listens and who writes down what they've heard as an aid to memory.

That's all fine. But what happens if you say: 'I encountered this person, we had a conversation,' and then add, 'It was an *ethnographic* encounter,' and 'I'm not just anyone, I'm an *ethnographer*. I wasn't merely having a conversation with a friend; I was *doing ethnography*'? What do you mean by that? It means, in a sense, that you have turned your back on this person. You are saying, 'I'm not just having a conversation with you because you and I are good friends, and we're interested in what each other is doing. I'm having a conversation with you because I want to get some information, which is going to be material for an account I'm intending to write up.' And that's where the problem arises. For most of us, while we're in the field, we're probably not too bothered by this. We just let life go by, and write everything down. The problem comes when we're done with all that and return home with our stash of fieldnotes. It's then that we turn round and declare, 'During all that time, I was an ethnographer, and look what I've got, here are my ethnographic data!' That changes the relationship completely. It is not just that you have left the community you were working with; you've actually turned your back on it, and all those things you learned from people have now become raw material for analysis. It turns out that all the time that you were *with* them, you were actually trying to collect information *on* them. That's why I think it is so problematic.

In practice, this implies that the 'ethno' in ethnography only comes to the fore after you've left the field. Perhaps, then, we should turn the prefix 'ethno' into a verb. What happens when you 'ethno' people, or 'ethno' a particular field of their activity? I've recently been in discussion with a group of colleagues talking about ethnomathematics, and there are all sorts of other 'ethno's out there: ethno-botany, ethno-science, ethno-medicine, ethno-this, ethno-that. What does this *ethno*-ing of things actually do? What it does is to take a body of discussion around certain themes – things people know, things people talk about – and package it up, as if to say: 'Right, this is part of the corpus that belongs to these people, this ethnos, as a kind of collective property. But it is now, at least partly, in my possession and I'm going to write it up. It will now be my ethnography.' I think this *ethno*-ing move is very dangerous. It comes in retrospect, when we're no longer with the people and subjected to the kinds of everyday pressures we experience when they are all around us. It is when we remove ourselves that they suddenly morph into this ethnos, this folk, to whom we go on to attribute all sorts of qualities. That's where the problem lies, and I've been trying to get anthropologists to think about it, because I believe the way we use 'ethnography' to refer interchangeably *both* to participant observation in the field, *and* to the work we do in writing up afterwards, has brushed it under the carpet.

Robert Gibb

In a recent commentary on anthropology and ethnography, you write: 'I should admit at the outset that the matters at stake in the troubled union of anthropology and ethnography are by no means as settled in my mind as they are on the page, and while I have endeavoured to set them out as clearly as I can, the long-running argument that I have been having with myself continues and shows no sign of abating.'[4] I was really intrigued by this, and was wondering if you could tell us more about the doubts, uncertainties and ambivalences you continue to experience.

Tim Ingold

Absolutely! Because I do have these doubts, all the time. The thing is that when you write something you have to come out with a position and argue for it, which is what I try to do. But I always have at the back of my mind the possibility that I could just as well have argued otherwise. I am by no means as convinced of my own position as I sound. To be honest, I still feel torn, not so much in discussions with anthropological colleagues as when I find myself explaining or justifying what we do to non-anthropologists. Much of the problem with the way we have been using the notion of ethnography is that it doesn't help people from outside anthropology to better understand what we actually do. We know that anthropology has a big problem when it comes to public understanding. The subject is terribly misunderstood, and I feel that projecting ourselves as ethnographers only makes matters worse.

---

4 See Ingold (2021a: 141).

If you find yourself in conversation with a philosopher, a cultural theorist, a political analyst or whatever, you soon discover that these people very rarely do anything akin to what we would call fieldwork. They spend most of their time reading the work of researchers who are doing the same as they are. They read lots of books and articles, engage in critique and attend conferences where they vigorously defend their positions amidst the fray. All of this is supposed to hold a mirror to the world, but it is a world they are reluctant ever to enter themselves. When you talk with them, you soon discover that they know next to nothing of what goes on *in* the world of which they profess such exalted insight, because it has never occurred to them to study in it. And that's the point. I would say to them: 'Look here, we anthropologists know a thing or two about what is going on in the world. Why? Because we do fieldwork! Just look at our ethnography!' Then I realise that, in saying this, I have made a perfectly good argument for why ethnography is so fundamental to anthropology, which goes right against the grain of what I said in response to your earlier question. It looks as if I'm directly contradicting myself!

For me, however, it all depends on whom I am talking to. With fellow anthropologists it is not so much of an issue because, call it what we will, we have a common unwritten understanding of what we're really up to, whether in the field or in writing up afterwards. But in conversations outside of anthropology the issue really hits me on the head, because I then have to explain that we know what we know precisely because we have been involved in so many conversations with so many people from different parts of the world with different experience. This is a lot of words. Could 'ethnography' simply be a less long-winded way of saying the same thing, in just one word? If you get into a debate with a theorist, and you want to point out that you are knowledgeable about something that's going on in the world, because you've talked to people and bothered to listen, you might say 'Look, it's in my ethnography!' It's a short-cut word for all that. The fact is, however, that it's not a good word, because it evokes this idea of the *ethnos*, the 'folk', the people, which is problematic in itself, not to mention *-graphy*, which is 'writing about'. Literally, ethnography means *writing about the people*. But for that reason, it is entirely ill-suited to capture the essence of anthropological inquiry, which is *with* rather than *about*, and not bound to any *ethnos*. Why use 'ethnography' to mean the very opposite of what it stands for?

Robert Gibb

In your original 2007 Radcliffe-Brown Lecture, and in subsequent contributions to the debate, you have stated that neither anthropology nor ethnography is 'prior to' or 'better than' the other; they are just different. Nevertheless, it could be argued that when you say that anthropologists 'do their thinking, talking and writing in and with the world', while the ethnographer 'retrospectively imagines a world from which he has *turned away* in order, quite specifically, that he might *describe it in writing*,'[5] you are making an implicit value judgement in favour of anthropology. How would you respond?

Tim Ingold

That's a fair criticism, and I have long worried about it myself. Maybe I'm guilty of double standards. There must be a certain value in detachment. Think about the resources we have. For example, in my work with northern circumpolar peoples, one of my most cherished sources is the classic account by Waldemar Bogoras, dating from the years 1904 to 1909, of the Chukchi people, indigenous to the northeastern tip of Siberia. Bogoras found himself in this remote region, at the turn of the twentieth century, as a political exile, and his account is based on many years of living with them. His enormous work, *The Chukchee*, originally published in three volumes, is packed with details of Chukchi life. I keep returning to it, and always find something new. Bogoras worked in what we would now regard as a very traditional way, collecting everything he could about the people

---

5 See Ingold (2008: 88, italics in the original).

and their ways. But now we have it; it's available as a resource, not only for us but also for Chukchi people themselves.

There is an intrinsic value to this, just as there is an intrinsic value to works like encyclopaedias. We now have a record of ways of life which may have either disappeared or changed beyond recognition – a record that we wouldn't otherwise have. That must be a good thing. Indeed it is, so long as we don't pretend it to be anything other than what it really is. It isn't part of an inquiry into the conditions and possibilities of human life. It simply documents, as accurately as it can. It doesn't pretend to be more than that and as such, it is not a means to the end of anthropology. It stands in its own right, I think, in a way comparable to the artefacts collected in a museum. Some might be critical of museum collecting, or the museumisation of material culture, which takes things out of context and packages them, arranging them into cases. But despite all of that, we wouldn't want to say that museums are a waste of time – that they serve no purpose. They do have a purpose to serve. And so does ethnography. On the one hand, we wouldn't want to be without it; but on the other, we shouldn't pretend that it is other than what it is.

Diego Maria Malara

Your 2014 paper on ethnography rests on a sharp distinction between anthropology and ethnography, as well as between participation and observation. In particular, ethnography as the actual writing of research experience is conceived as a decidedly retrospective operation, something that one does at home, generally with the goal of publishing a piece. It seems to me that to make this point you have to rely on a model of research that might not match the experience of many anthropologists. Importantly, data collection, interpretation (even if tentative) and writing are, to an extent, often simultaneous practices for many researchers (see Shyrock 2016). So why do you think that we should maintain the temporal (and spatial) divides that underpin this conception of ethnography as a *fait accompli* operation? Is this a distinction that you have extrapolated from your own research experience?

Tim Ingold

Well, in my own experience, and I think that of others too, the sort of writing we do with fieldnotes is completely different from the kind of writing we do when we write an article, a thesis or a book based on those notes. It's a quite different business. The kind of writing we do in the field is very similar to letter-writing or writing a diary. We are not really pulling stuff together. You might make a note of what you need to do tomorrow, what questions need to be asked next. But you remain very local, very situated, all the while thinking: 'Following the journey so far, what are my next steps?' So long as you remain in the field, you can never have a synoptic view of things. You cannot possibly gain such a view, since you are in the thick of it. Not until you finish, can you see what happened early on in your fieldwork in the light of what happened later on. You can't do that while it's still going on. So there is a shift of perspective, which takes its time.

I'm sure you've heard the adage that for the first three months or so after returning from fieldwork, you are 'too close to the field' to write anything coherent. You have to get your head around things after returning from the field, before you can even begin writing. And while this is happening, you can usefully spend time digesting and organising your fieldnotes in a way that makes them manageable. As you read and think them through again, things begin to take shape, to form a pattern. Only then can you begin writing. But this writing could not be more different from the kind you do in the field. Field writing is prospective, and in that sense temporally on a par with everything else going on. You are conversing, you are participating in everyday activities, you are writing a diary. It's all part of a daily routine. The writing that you do later on – the 'writing up', as we say – is an altogether different task. It is retrospective rather than prospective. It's a mere accident that we use the same word for both.

Robert Gibb

As you explained in the Radcliffe-Brown lecture, one of your aims in initiating a debate about ethnography and anthropology was to liberate ethnography from what you called 'the tyranny of method'.[6] You appear to have a similar aim in relation to participant observation, as in a 2016 interview with Susan MacDougall, in which you insisted 'that participant-observation is not a research method but, more fundamentally, an ontological commitment: an acknowledgement of our debt to the world for who we are and what we know'. Please could you say a little more about the argument you are making here. In particular, if participant observation is an 'ontological commitment' rather than 'a research method', is it something we can 'teach' our students as part of their preparations for fieldwork? If so, how? And how can we argue for such a view of participant observation in the face of pressure from institutions and funders to provide 'research methods training'?

Tim Ingold

This is a big one! My first inclination is to say no, you can't teach what is, in fact, the ontological commitment that underpins the practice of teaching itself. To try to teach it would be to turn this commitment into its own object. The apprentice woodworker learns woodwork through apprenticeship, not apprenticeship through woodwork. Likewise, I don't think that you can teach participant observation as such, and I don't believe it has ever really been taught. All that anybody can do in practice is tell students about their own experiences, about how they learned things through their own apprenticeship to masters in the field, in the particular and probably unique set of circumstances in which they found themselves, knowing full well that everyone else is going to find themselves in different circumstances. The idea that there is a rule book to follow, or that participant observation can be formally operationalised, is

---

6 See Ingold (2008: 88).

absurd. But it's an absurdity put about by funders, research councils and so on. I think this has to do with professionalisation. Over the last two or three decades, the practice and vocation of research has been hooked up to a model of the professional as expert. And the professional expert has to be qualified and accredited, which means they have to demonstrate that they are in possession of technical qualifications that non-professionals lack. Hence the need for formal accreditation.

I recently read up on this and discovered that the 'curriculum vitae', as we know it today, is a rather new phenomenon. It scarcely existed before the 1980s, when it suddenly took off. It was part of the trend towards the marketisation of skills that really got going at that time, and has been with us ever since. Nowadays, to get a job, everyone needs a CV. So, if your research is intended to help you build a professional career, and if research councils are disbursing the funds that enable you to do so, then you have to end up with something to put on your CV. Prior to that, the researcher was understood basically as an amateur – in the literal sense, meaning that they would do their research for the love of it. For them it wasn't a way of staging a career; it was simply a way of living a good life. It could be living a good life with books, or by spending time with whatever you are interested in. Of course, this had its own problems, because it meant that only those with independent means could actually do it. The great naturalists of the nineteenth century, Charles Darwin included, were all 'gentleman scholars', and they had the money to do whatever they wanted. Their studies were amateur rather than professional, in today's sense of what being professional means. What has happened since is that research methods have become akin to professional qualifications, something to put on your CV. And the result is that they have, to a degree, been fetishised.

But you could tackle the question another way, by looking more closely at what the word 'method' actually means. Literally, it means 'the way beyond', from the classical Greek *hodos* ('way') plus *meta* ('beyond'). Thus, a method is a way of going beyond where you are now. And 'research'? It means to search and search again, in which every new search both doubles up on what you did before and, in the process, takes you beyond where you were. Taken literally, then, both 'method' and 'research' mean pretty much the same thing. Research is method; and method is research. And if that's what we mean by research and by method, then I am absolutely fine with it. It's the path we take to seek a way beyond where we are now.

But as soon as these two things, research and method, become hooked to a ladder of professional qualification, they immediately descend into the nonsense typical of the research proposals we are required to submit to funding bodies, in which we try to pretend that in carrying out our research, we deliberately apply certain prescribed methodological protocols. To take just one invidious example of this kind of nonsense: instead of talking with whoever happens to pass by, and following up if they suggest other useful leads, we propose to apply what is known as a 'snowball technique'. This comes to exactly the same thing, of course, but makes it sound more methodological. We all know, indeed, that what we actually do is not what we say on the research proposal. We need to say one thing in order to get the money, then we go into the field and do something altogether different. We all know that. So we are having to get by with what I would call 'tolerated mendacity', and I don't think this is a good place to be. I wish we could find a way to be more truthful. But it's extremely awkward when what is involved is the distribution of public funds. It was easy so long as everybody had the means to do whatever they wanted, but that is no longer the case. And, to be honest, I don't know what the solution is.

Diego Maria Malara

In your paper 'That's enough about ethnography', you tell us that there is an issue with ethnography, and you propose an original framing. One cannot help wondering about methods, about the practicalities of being in the field, such as taking notes. You say very little about these things, both in the paper as well as in other works. You seem to tell us that there is an issue, and a big one, with how anthropologists do things, but there are no substantive suggestions on how things can and should be done. Or, better, your suggestions tend to be quite abstract. Could you tell us something more about your views on the concrete aspects of fieldwork, how you do it and what advice would you give to a student who is about to leave for his or her field today?

Tim Ingold

True, I haven't written much about it. But I have lost count of the number of times I have *spoken* about it, mainly in conversation with students. I have talked endlessly about my research and how I did it. As everyone's circumstances are so different, however, this is better done in conversation than in print. The thing is that my fieldwork was done in pre-digital days; everything had to be done by hand. I couldn't type; I am still a hopeless typist! The key thing, and the most important message I try to get across to every student, is the importance of writing comprehensive fieldnotes. It's as simple as that. Writing notes involves time, discipline, concentration, and it is incredibly hard work. Sometimes you will be up all night writing, while everyone else is asleep. Students need to realise this. They need to know that there is more to fieldwork than just participating in things, taking photos and jotting down the odd note in the evening. Writing fieldnotes is time-consuming and extremely laborious.

That's the first thing I tell them. 'Never imagine,' I say, 'that events that seem unforgettable at the time, that even seem to change your life, will stay that way. A couple of years later, you will have forgotten all about them. Picture yourself sitting in your study, in a completely different environment, and trying to write based on what you remember. If you have failed at the time to write everything down, you will later be wringing your hands in despair. For there's no other way of bringing things back. And because, at the time of occurrence, you have no idea what will turn out to be important in retrospect, and what will not, it is essential to get everything down, everything you have observed. You will need to write pages and pages and pages of notes.'

The other thing I tell students is that there's no point in having a system of notation and record-keeping which turns out to be unmanageable once you have finished in the field and begin to use it. For example, it's no use thinking that you can avoid taking notes simply by recording everything on some kind of device, because you would then have to spend the next ten years transcribing all the recordings, even before having anything to work on. There's absolutely no substitute for proper old-fashioned fieldnotes.

The technique I developed was to write on very thin paper. I could mount four sheets on a clipboard, with three sheets of carbon paper in between. I would write with a ballpoint pen, pressing hard, in a very small hand to economise on paper, and in that way, I would instantly get three copies. The last copy was difficult to read, but that was my insurance copy, which I would post at intervals to my supervisor. I would have it as a backup, in case anything got lost. I kept the top copy intact. But I spent the first two or three months after returning from the field cutting the second and third copies into strips, with scissors, which I glued with Pritt Stick onto backing paper. I arranged these glued strips into two files, one organised by the household to which the people mentioned in the snippet belonged, the other by the activity in question: reindeer herding, fishing, local politics and so on. This meant that if I needed to find out anything about particular people I could immediately do so, by consulting the relevant entry in the household file; and likewise with the other file, if I wanted to check on any particular activity.

And it worked! It took me three months after returning from the field to organise my materials, in the course of which I read everything through, very carefully. Maybe researchers are doing the same thing now as I did, only using digital means; they can easily use a search function to track down what they need. There are shortcuts available now that weren't available then. But I sometimes wonder whether these shortcuts are such a good thing, because they don't force you to reflect on your materials as I had to do. Working by hand with scissors and glue, I think I gained a feel for the material that I would not otherwise have done, had I been working solely at a keyboard.

There's one more thing I would tell every student. The point about fieldnotes, I would tell them, is not that they are a compendium of data for analysis. Rather, they are a mnemonic aid. They enable you to sit in your study, busily writing, and to be back there in the field, at one and the same time. It's extraordinary! When you reread your fieldnotes, even after the lapse of years, it is as if it had all happened only yesterday. And because it's really fresh in your mind, you can write about it in a way that you would not have been able to do otherwise. These are things that you learn from experience and that can be easily explained. It is what I did in my fieldwork, in concrete, practical terms, and it is the advice I would offer to any student intending to carry out fieldwork today.

(D) ANTHROPOLOGY AND/AS EDUCATION

Philip Tonner

What is the role (beyond just influences) of past thinkers, such as John Dewey, on your educational and anthropological thinking?

Tim Ingold

I came upon Dewey absurdly late. I really didn't read his work properly until I had to give the Dewey lectures, on which my education book is based, and when I did, I was astonished. We are all expected to wade through the writings of Marx, Weber, Durkheim and the rest. Why not Dewey? Why is his work not on every undergraduate reading list? It is not, and I don't know why. It's a curious thing, because I believe Dewey's thought is incredibly relevant to our times and, in many ways, an advance on the sort of sociological thinking to which we are normally treated from the masters, the grandfathers of our discipline.

Some years ago, in 2014, I had to write a short piece for the *Journal of the Royal Anthropological Institute*, 'A Life in Books', for which I was asked to choose the five books that I felt had had the greatest influence on my thinking, and to write a paragraph on each. The first on my list was naturally Henri Bergson's *Creative Evolution*. I was reading Bergson in the early 1980s, long before he came back into fashion, as has increasingly happened today. I came across *Creative Evolution* more or less by accident, but it blew my mind. Bergson was already saying everything I wanted to say. His has been a huge influence for me. I often find myself saying things that come directly from his writings, but which have become so much a part of my own thinking that I had forgotten that this was where they originally came from. Second on my list was James Gibson's *The Ecological Approach to the Visual Perception*, which I also came across by accident, following the advice of the prominent ecological psychologist Ed Reed.[7] Gibson's approach turned out to be fundamental to the way I was trying to rethink ecological anthropology. Next was Merleau-Ponty's *Phenomenology of Perception*. I never set out to be a phenomenologist, but I discovered this work because I was interested in perception, and it helped me resolve some doubts I was having with Gibson's take on it. Then, as part of my engagement with evolutionary biology, I read a book by the philosopher Susan Oyama, *The Ontogeny of Information*. It's a terribly neglected work, but I consider it to be one of the most important ever written in the philosophy of biology. It was foundational to the perceptual-cum-developmental approach I was trying to develop. My fifth choice was André Leroi-Gourhan's *Gesture and Speech*. Leroi-Gourhan was a veritable polymath, a student of Marcel Mauss, working across the history of technology, archaeology and prehistoric art. The breadth of his vision was incredible: completely chaotic, but very inspiring.

7 I have described my encounter with Reed in Conversation 1.

These, then, were the five books that have had the greatest influence on me. And what is interesting about them is that with the possible exception of Leroi-Gourhan's, none is specifically anthropological. I never found that depth of inspiration from my reading in anthropology, although as a student in Cambridge I was much influenced by Edmund Leach and learned a good deal from both Meyer Fortes and Jack Goody. I have learned from plenty of people, but their influence was not formative in the sense of actually making me change the way I think about things. I think this says something, because if you were to ask what works have been most influential for the development of specifically anthropological theory over the past few decades, it is unlikely that any of my choices would be included in the list.

Philip Tonner

You've also argued for something of an equivalence between anthropology and education. Can you explain your reasoning for this?

Tim Ingold

It means having to think about education in a particular way. In my book *Anthropology and/as Education*, based on the Dewey lectures, I argued against the standard transmission model of education – that there is a body of knowledge to be transferred from adults who know to children who don't – and for an idea of education as a way of *leading life*, as a way of taking oneself out of one's existing standpoint so as to experience the world directly, with a certain intensity, and to learn from it. Besides Dewey, I was engaging in particular with the work of two contemporary educational theorists: Gert Biesta and Jan Masschelein. Though their approaches differ in many ways, they have in common a desire to think of education as a practice of what the former calls 'weak' and the latter 'poor' pedagogy. By way of contrast, a 'strong' or 'rich' pedagogy would be one that has a body of authoritative knowledge to transfer. It would arm us with this knowledge, offering a protective shield in the battle against adversity in an inherently competitive environment. But weak pedagogy, for Biesta, is a process of *disarmament*; while for Masschelein, poor pedagogy is a process of *exposure*. Instead of shoring ourselves up with knowledge so that we can defend ourselves against adversaries, it strips our defences away, leaving us so exposed that we can actually notice our fellow beings in the world, attend to them and learn from them. Both Biesta and Masschelein are trying to elaborate on the meaning of education in this sense.

I found this really exciting, since it immediately occurred to me that this is exactly what we're doing in anthropology! Fieldwork is precisely a practice of exposure in Masschelein's sense – of being pulled 'out of position' – or what Biesta calls disarmament. You arrive in a place and think: 'I don't know anything, but I'm here to learn, by paying attention to what people do and say.' It's sometimes uncomfortable; it's risky, and there is no clear body of knowledge to be acquired, but you discover a lot about both yourself and the world in the process. It seemed to me, then, that what anthropology is doing in the posture of fieldwork, and what education in this weak or poor sense is doing, are pretty much the same thing. It would follow, therefore, not only that anthropology can provide a model for how this kind of education could work, but also that the role of anthropology in our society could be regarded as fundamentally educative. That's how I came to the view that the first priority, in anthropology, must be educational rather than ethnographic. We're not here to describe or catalogue other people's lives; we're here to open ourselves up to them. If we understand education in this sense, then that's what we do in anthropology. At least, it is what we *should* be doing; it should be our top priority.

Philip Tonner

Education, for you, is to open yourself up to a way of living with others, being responsive to them and to your shared world, of attending to things in terms of process. Education is about opening, to quote you again, paths of discovery and growth. Given this, what advice, perhaps based on your own experience as an educator, would you give to teachers who would wish to develop your thinking in their practice?

Tim Ingold

The first word of advice I would give to a teacher is to assume that the students you are teaching are as intelligent as you are: *never ever* talk down to them, never say that learning is easy or try and make it any less difficult for them. Instead, present things in all their difficulty and say: 'Look, this is a struggle, and it takes effort. I'm not going to make things easy for you, but I'm going to respect your intelligence and understand that you are just as capable of understanding as I am, although maybe you haven't read all the things I have.' That would be the first thing.

Then, just explain that the point about the teacher is not that they've got the knowledge and the students haven't, because this would simply reproduce the image of the student as ignorant – and students are not ignorant. Aim instead to be a constant companion, someone to whom students can always turn for guidance, for advice, for assistance and for careful criticism. Read what students write, listen to what they say and respond in your own voice, as best you can – but don't claim always to have the answers. The idea is to take students along with you, like going on an expedition where you have no more idea than anyone else of where, if anywhere, it will fetch up. That, I think, is what good teaching is.

Diego Maria Malara

You have written, Tim, that 'More than any other discipline in the human sciences, [anthropology] has the means and the determination to show how knowledge grows from the crucible of lives lived with others.'[8] We find this formulation particularly intriguing. Could you explain what this means in relation to your suggestion that we don't simply study our interlocutors, we study *with* them?

Tim Ingold

Let me return to the start of the passage you quoted: 'More than any other discipline in the human sciences . . .' That's critical. It returns us to something we discussed earlier. If we were to compare anthropology with other disciplines that work in one way or another with human subjects, anthropology is the only one, I believe, which actually listens to what people say or do in its own right, rather than simply treating it as data. We listen to what people tell us, rather than for what it tells us about them. In my little book *Anthropology: Why It Matters*, I have called this 'taking others seriously'. Other disciplines, even in the humanities and social sciences, are not really doing that. It's because we take people seriously that the knowledge coming out of our work grows, and is grown, from these conversations. That's what I mean by 'the crucible of lives lived with others'. If we go to study *with* other people, it is because they have wisdom and experience from which we could potentially learn; it might help us all, collectively, in our future endeavours. That's why we do anthropology, in my view.

Diego Maria Malara

OK, so here's a very basic question, Tim. What does anthropology offer to an 18-year-old student today?

Tim Ingold

I think it offers the possibility to reflect seriously on the big questions of how to live in a way that engages with real life. If I were an

8 See Ingold (2014a: 387).

18-year-old today, I would be intensely worried about the state of the world. I'd be worrying about climate change, about the environment, about authoritarian regimes, about violence, about the military, about poverty. I'd have hundreds of things to be desperately worried about. I would not be so naïve as to suppose that there's any one discipline out there that can provide all the answers, but I would want to find some space in which it is possible to think and to reflect seriously on all these issues in a way that is rigorous and informed and, most importantly, in touch with people's lives. If you were to review all the possible disciplines in which to study, I think you would find that anthropology is the only discipline that offers such a space. So that's what I would say to the 18-year-old. Disciplines like philosophy, politics and economics have different priorities. Anthropology, I think, is the most exciting and intellectually challenging, precisely because of the wealth of human experience it embraces.

Robert Gibb

And is that, do you think, what would distinguish anthropology from, say, sociology?

Tim Ingold

That's a tricky question, as you know, because sociology itself is so riven. You're caught between the data crunchers, the positivists, who in many ways still rule the roost, and the arch-theorists who consider themselves above such things. It has always seemed to me that the recent history of sociology is almost entirely bound up with positivism and what to do about it. You are either for it or against it. And whichever side you take, sociology continues to carve out the domain of the social from everything else in ways that I find extremely problematic. Anthropology doesn't do that. The thing about anthropology, as we've always said, is that it doesn't concentrate on any particular slice of human life. Sociology deals with society; theology with religion; economics with the economy; politics with the state.

But anthropology deals with the whole lot. It starts with humanity unsliced. And that, I think, is one of its great virtues.

(E) THE 'RECLAIMING OUR UNIVERSITY' MOVEMENT

Robert Gibb

Our final questions today are about the 'Reclaiming Our University' movement at the University of Aberdeen. How did you become involved with this and what do you think some of the effects of the movement, notably its manifesto, have been, both at the University of Aberdeen itself and more widely?

Tim Ingold

Well, that's a long story, but what happened was that the University was going through a crisis. We had a failing management; morale was very low; and there were cuts or threatened cuts everywhere. This was in 2015. Things were getting really bad and colleagues, both from my own Department and from other parts of the University, kept coming to me and saying: 'Tim, what are you going to do about this?' I thought: 'Why are they coming to me?' I think it was because I was considered bulletproof. Colleagues at that time were genuinely worried that if they raised their voices in any sort of criticism, they would end up being eased out of their jobs, as indeed happened in many cases. So, they were too nervous to speak out. But they thought I could, because I was senior and there would have been a scandal if they had tried to kick me out.

I had a lot of meetings over the summer of 2015, in coffee shops, which would often end with the words 'This meeting never took place!' In a way it was quite exciting cloak-and-dagger stuff, which was new to me. We decided to do things in the traditional way. I had posters printed and we stuck them on lampposts and walls around the campus. It was a race to get them up before the authorities pulled them down. We convened a meeting out of hours, in a church hall just off the campus, to discuss three questions: 'What kind of university do we want?', 'How should it operate?' and 'How should we achieve it?' Two hundred people turned up, including some from management, who stood at the back, taking names. Then we discussed the problem of what to do next. We decided to arrange a series of seminars which would be open to all: students, staff, everyone. These focused on what we saw as the four pillars of the university: *freedom*, *trust*, *education* and *community*. They were lively events, and they culminated in the production of our manifesto, launched in November 2016. By summer of 2017 our Principal, Ian Diamond, was out and we got an entirely new management team, which professed to be enthusiastic about the manifesto and committed to its principles. It's been doing reasonably well within the limits of what is possible, especially given the difficult situation all universities are in just now. Eventually, the Reclaiming Our University movement in Aberdeen was disbanded, on the grounds that it had fulfilled its purpose. We won the battle, though perhaps not the war.

What we proved was that this sort of thing is possible, but only if it is done from the ground up; it has to be a local movement. Similar movements have been underway in many other universities, with differing degrees of success. It sometimes feels like turning an oil tanker, but I think it's the only way to revive our universities for generations to come. It could be that the current crisis, the ongoing pandemic, will hasten some sort of change. But the situation across the university sector is generally dire, especially in England, where universities are hugely in debt, or have built prestigious buildings on which they will have to pay interest. They will end up either going bankrupt or having to lay off staff in order to pay for empty buildings. The situation is manifestly unsustainable. But you do find much more open public questioning of the marketisation agenda than even as little as two or three years ago. And that's a hopeful sign.

Robert Gibb

What struck me about what you said is the importance of a bottom-up movement, but also one in which professors like you are involved. People are very scared, aren't they?

Tim Ingold

People are indeed scared, and they have good reason to be so. I was even a little scared myself. These were tense times. I am astonished by how many people in my position, either retired, close to retirement, senior or well established, are not doing anything. They're sitting in high places, having learned discussions, meeting with important people, sitting on committees, giving each other honours. But they're doing absolutely nothing. It's really depressing, the lack of leadership from my level. I find it sad. These people are perfectly well aware of the problems of precarity, of how difficult it is for the younger generation of scholars. Do they do anything about it? No, because they can rest on their laurels. I get very angry about this.

Diego Maria Malara

What do you think are the biggest institutional obstacles to overcoming the problems we've been talking about?

Tim Ingold

It's really difficult. The thing is that many people have lost sight of what universities are *for*. In a way, that's the biggest obstacle. The purpose of universities is not to cultivate a meritocratic and cosmopolitan elite, or to reproduce the global knowledge economy, or to support business, or to make Britain more productive. There is no well-formulated alternative because we currently lack a proper idea of what the purpose of education is, in relation to creating a future for coming generations. I think that's the problem. You cannot have institutional change unless you're crystal-clear about what it's changing to, and why.

We need to define the meaning and purpose of higher education in the contemporary world, so as to offer a coherent and convincing alternative to the neoliberal business model. This means putting the emphasis, just as Dewey did in his 1916 masterpiece, *Democracy and Education*, on the importance of an educated citizenship for democracy. We made the same point in the first paragraphs of our manifesto. You cannot have a mature democracy without educated citizens. Educating citizens is an intergenerational necessity. It is a collective, moral and ethical task, from which everyone should stand to benefit, not just a meritocratic few. These things need to be clearly formulated. Only then can we chart a way forward. Rather than destroying the institutions we have, or allowing them to destroy themselves by going bankrupt, we can instead steer them in a direction which offers hope for the future.

The changes required are enormous. They have a lot to do, for example, with relationships between universities and the communities or regions in which they are situated. With the current emphasis on international rankings, the ways universities can be of service to their communities and regions have been all but ignored. They are accorded little value, beyond local marketing campaigns. This needs to be reversed. We have to start thinking about universities in rather the same way that we think about public libraries, as places where anyone can go for any period, and at any time of life, to enhance their knowledge or wisdom in some area that matters to them. We have to rethink the purpose of university education and scholarship in terms of their contribution to the common good.

There is, however, one major obstacle which we encountered with the Reclaiming movement, and it is still there. That obstacle is what we could call 'big science'. I don't mean all scientists. I mean the kind of science that depends on massive investments and huge infrastructure projects, for example the Large Hadron Collider, or the aerospace facilities for sending rockets to the moon. This kind of big science not only has a blinkered vision of the future, which revolves around escaping the planet rather than inhabiting it. It is also absolutely committed to, and reliant on, the business model of education, research and development, with its obsessions with technological innovation, artificial intelligence and so on. Big science has its hands on the levers of power, while we in the arts, humanities and social sciences are relegated to the scrap heap. This is a real problem. One way to tackle it would be for those of us working in the arts, humanities and social sciences to be much clearer than we generally are about the purposes and potentials of our own scholarship. We need to show why it is so fundamental. Even science depends upon it; indeed, I would argue that at the present juncture, we alone can save big science from itself, from its destructive, escapist and totalitarian instincts. We are nowhere near there yet. There's so much to be done.

Further Reading

The first six debates organised by the GDAT were edited by Ingold and published in 1996 under the title *Key Debates in Anthropology*. His 'General Introduction' to the volume (Ingold 1996b) includes a discussion of the nature and role of theory in anthropology. As noted in the interview, Ingold reflects on the place of 'politics' in his work in an article, subtitled 'towards a politics of dwelling', published in 2005. Examples of recent work sympathetic to Ingold's general approach, but arguing that it pays insufficient attention to questions of political economy, include Hornborg (2018) and Howard (2018).

On the question of difference versus diversity, Ingold refers in the interview to Leach's 1967 Reith Lectures, *A Runaway World?* (Leach 1967). Ingold offers a critical reflection on Leach's argument in the second chapter of his *Anthropology: Why It Matters* (Ingold 2018a),

Ingold lists the five books that have influenced him most in 'A Life in Books' (Ingold 2014a). The five are Bergson's *Creative Evolution* (1911), Gibson's *The Ecological Approach to Visual Perception* (1979), Merleau-Ponty's *Phenomenology of Perception* (1962), Oyama's *The Ontogeny of Information* (1985) and Leroi-Gourhan's *Gesture and Speech* (1993).

On the difference between anthropology and ethnography, see, inter alia, Ingold (2008, 2014a). For a range of different perspectives on this question, see the special issue of the journal *HAU* (da Col, ed. 2017) and the recent collection edited by Ahmad (2021). On professionalisation and how it has affected the status of ethnography, see Ingold (2021c). The relationship between anthropology and education is explored in Ingold's book *Anthropology and/as Education* (2018a), and more recently in his edited volume *Knowing from the Inside* (2022b). In his discussion of the meaning of education, Ingold refers to the classic work of Dewey (1966), and contemporary writing by both Biesta (2006, 2013) and Masschelein (2010a, 2010b). The Manifesto of the Reclaiming Our University movement is available online at: https://reclaimingouruniversity.wordpress.com/.

CONVERSATION 3:

Environment, perception and skill

> **Summary:** This conversation explores some of the key ideas and arguments Ingold developed in *The Perception of the Environment* (2000), an influential collection of essays that has stimulated much debate, not only within anthropology but also in many other disciplines and fields of study. In the first part, Ingold outlines his perspective on the perception of the environment and discusses some of the key concepts he has used, notably 'the mycelial person', 'landscape', 'taskscape', 'dwelling' and 'habitation'. He also reflects on how his work relates to current developments in environmental debates about sustainability and the 'global climate crisis'. The second and third parts of the interview focus on Ingold's writing on 'materiality' and 'skill', respectively, and provide an accessible and stimulating introduction to these two key themes in his work. In this conversation Ingold also discusses at some length how reading Marx's work helped him develop his ideas. The interview took place on 12 August 2021.

(A) THE PERCEPTION OF THE ENVIRONMENT

Diego Maria Malara

The Perception of the Environment is a collection of your essays that addresses rather diverse topics, and at times it's quite difficult to detect a unifying thread. What lay behind the book and what were the key arguments you made in it?

Tim Ingold

Maybe the first thing to say is that originally *The Perception of the Environment* was intended to be three separate books. I collected all these essays and I thought: 'There's going to be a book about livelihood, mostly about hunting and gathering; and then there'll be a book about perceiving environments and landscapes; and then there'll be a book about technology and skill.' The publisher very sensibly persuaded me to put them all together in one. They said that if I published three books, they would end up competing with one another. Prospective readers would buy just one, and ignore the other two. It would be much better to publish them all between two covers. But perhaps that's also why, as you say, it's quite hard to find a unifying thread that links them all. In a sense, there's a thread for each of the parts of the book, but they are still to some extent separate from one another. That is just because of the way the whole thing was assembled.

Behind the book was my dissatisfaction with a number of approaches coming from biology, psychology and philosophy. Though they arrived by various routes, all are ultimately traceable to Kant or Descartes. Common to them all was the idea that human beings on the one hand, and their environments on the other, can be treated as separate entities which would then interact. I wanted to construct an alternative to the dominant synthesis formed of Cartesian philosophy, cognitive science, neo-Darwinian biology and the rather orthodox kind of cultural theory that was still prevalent in anthropology. That was the dominant synthesis at the time.

What all those approaches had in common was the a priori separation of the individual human being, as a living, thinking subject, from the environment in which it lives. It seemed to me that it is an existential condition of life for a being to *inhabit* a world, and I wanted to develop an alternative that would unite phenomenology – which starts from this assumption of being-in-the-world – with developmental biology, ecological psychology and a relational approach in anthropology. I thought that if I could put these together, I could then build a much better synthesis than the dominant one consisting of cognitivism, neo-Darwinism and so forth. That's really what I was trying to do.

So far as the social sciences are concerned, I have always felt them to be somewhat marginal to the whole enterprise, and in a way I still do. Of course, that's a little unfair – you can't tar all the social sciences with the same brush; but the thing that makes anthropology distinct for me is that it has not sliced up human life into different levels, as if to say 'here's the sociological level; here's the psychological level; here's the biological level.' For me, the point of an anthropological approach is to refute this idea of different levels. If we're to talk about human existence, then you have to regard it as all-in-one. The problem I still see with the social sciences is that they presuppose the existence of a distinct domain, which you could call 'the social', and which social scientists profess to study, as against domains of other kinds: linguistic, biological, psychological and so forth.

I don't know whether there's a path to redemption for the social sciences. If you look at their history, it seems that much of it turns around the debate over positivism, the great debate about whether or not there can be such a thing as a science of society. There's a whole range of views, on a spectrum from strongly *for* positivism to strongly *against* it. Sociologists are still so mired in this debate; it's hard for them to move on from it. But anthropology, I think, has largely sidestepped the issue, to its great advantage.

Philip Tonner

You explore a notion of the 'mycelial person' in your work, and you relate this not only to comparing the person to the fungal mycelium, as a bundle of lines or relations along which life is lived; you also connect this idea to the disciplines of anthropology and to the biological sciences, in terms of its potential for subversion. When did you start to formulate these ideas and where do you stand in relation to them now? And do you perceive any connection in your thinking here to what has been called either 'postmodern' or 'post-structuralist' theory?

Tim Ingold

Well, the image of the mycelium, as you know, goes back to my childhood and as the son of a mycologist, I was bound to draw on it. It always struck me that mycology is a subversive discipline within the context of the botanical sciences, because fungi just don't behave in the way that organisms are supposed to behave. It seems to me that anthropologists, who tend to take a very relational view of things, are subversive of the mainstream social sciences in much the same way.

I first formulated the idea of the mycelial person sometime in the mid-1990s. It kind of grew on me. Then I started thinking about lines. Obviously, if you're thinking about people as bundles of lines, the mycelial image fits rather well. Then I noticed that Gilles Deleuze and Félix Guattari, in their sprawling meditation *A Thousand Plateaus*, were drawing on the image of the rhizome, and they were using it to mean pretty much the same thing. I prefer the mycelium, as I think it's botanically more accurate. So, where they talk about rhizomatic thinking, I talk about mycelial thinking, but we're basically on the same page.

I don't really relate my thinking to postmodernism. Though it was all the rage when the whole modernist thing began to collapse, I think it has virtually run out of steam by now. The whole point about postmodernism was that it wasn't anything in particular; it was just a kind of licence to try out anything you want. Some experiments were silly, and some weren't, but nearly all were self-indulgent and, thankfully,

I think we've moved beyond them. Not many nowadays would want to stand up and identify themselves as 'postmodern'. They might even feel a little embarrassed to do so. They might call themselves poststructuralists, and if they were identifying poststructuralism with a basically Deleuzean, neo-vitalist, neo-animist cast of thought, then I'm in the same ballpark, so to speak. I always go back to Bergson, whose ideas are centrally implicated in all of this. I'm quite attracted to the idea of bringing a kind of vitalism back into our thinking. If you call that poststructuralism, then I guess I'm in! But some thirty years have passed between the early days of poststructuralism and the present. The truth is that I don't find this labelling of currents of thinking particularly helpful. I just think about what I do, and never mind what school of thought, if any, it belongs to.

Diego Maria Malara

Your essay of 1993, 'The Temporality of the Landscape', which is rightfully considered one of your most influential, suggests an alternative to the dualistic perspectives that populate academic cosmologies. Could you explain your main argument with reference to the concept of landscape, the dwelling perspective and the taskscape?

Tim Ingold

I first wrote that paper during 1992, at what was personally a difficult time. I was going through a period of rather deep depression, which made it extremely hard to write.

Archaeologists, of course, had always been talking about landscape, and it had long been a central concept in art history and human geography as well. Up until then, however, it had figured rather little in anthropology. But around that time, in the early 1990s, several anthropologists began to pick up on the idea, and to think about what a specifically anthropological approach to landscape might be.

A flurry of articles and books on landscape followed, and I needed to sit down with them to work out a view of my own. The reason I needed to do so was that I had been preoccupied, until then, with the concept of environment, while also teaching a course in the field of ecological anthropology, in which the concept is pivotal. The problem for me – the question I was asking myself – was: what, if anything, is the difference between what I mean by *environment* and what others are calling *landscape*? Are we talking about the same thing, but just using different terms, or is there some fundamental difference between the two, between environment and landscape?

Initially, since the concept of environment had come out of ecology, it seemed to be biased towards a natural science perspective, whereas the concept of landscape, having been appropriated by the art historians, implied a perspective that came more from the humanities. For me, the question was: how can we get beyond this division between the natural sciences and the humanities? Could we find a place where the two perspectives would converge? Could we find a way of talking about our surroundings that would not be split between humanistic and scientific approaches? That was the challenge. In line with how I was thinking at the time, I decided that the way to address this was to think processually – to imagine a world not as if it were already laid out for us to perceive, to value aesthetically, perhaps to analyse and write about, but as perpetually coming into being around us. If you think in this way, then the question of time must obviously come into it. Whatever it is – landscape or environment or whatever else you want to call it – time must somehow enter into its constitution. I invented the concept of taskscape initially to deal with this. Ultimately, however, I wanted to show that if landscape *itself* is understood as a temporally unfolding phenomenon, then landscape and taskscape are one, and we no longer have need of a separate concept of taskscape at all. I introduced the concept, in short, precisely in order to get rid of it. That, anyway, was the general idea.

Around the year 1990, I was presenting one part of the introductory course in social anthropology to first-year undergraduate students at the University of Manchester. I wanted to convey to these students, who were encountering anthropology for the first time, what it means to study social life. I found a wonderful painting by Pieter Bruegel the Elder, 'The Fight between Carnival and Lent' (1559), which shows a market scene in sixteenth-century Flanders. The scene is packed with people doing all manner of things. I projected a slide of this picture and announced: 'Look, that is social life! All these people, they're all doing things: there are people buying and selling, there's a troop performing a play, there's a couple copulating, there's somebody begging. All sorts of stuff is going on.' But the painting is not of a landscape, at least in the conventional sense. What, then, is it a painting of? 'It's a painting of a taskscape,' I said, 'because there are all these people doing things. They've all got their different tasks, but they are carried on not in isolation but in relation to one another.' It had dawned on me that this is the way to explain to students what we are studying, when we say we study social life. We study the taskscape.

But then I switched my attention to another of Bruegel's paintings, 'The Harvesters' (1565). It is one of a series of paintings that Bruegel made for each month of the year, many of which are now lost. 'The Harvesters' is for the month of August. It's one of my favourite paintings, and a reproduction of the original, now housed in New York's Metropolitan Museum of Art, hangs on my study wall. Here in this painting is much more of what we would conventionally call landscape, with hills and valleys, trees and fields, a scattering of buildings and a distant shore. It is a rural scene, with only a few people.

The two paintings, 'The Harvesters' and 'The Fight between Carnival and Lent', were painted only a few years apart. Let's compare them. One I have called a landscape; the other a taskscape. But why? What's the difference? Only that the latter is crowded with people doing things, while the former is mostly scenery. But if we place both into the current of time, we realise that the lives and activities of the people are nested within the lives of trees and buildings, which are nested within the lives of hills, and so on. Temporally, everything is nested within everything else. Once this is acknowledged, we can bring these two ideas together, of landscape and taskscape, to find a holistic way of talking about the process.

The issue was: how we can we think of not just human beings, but everything else as well, as part of such a process, which we can follow only by taking up a position from the inside of its unfolding? That's where the dwelling perspective came in. It is the perspective I adopted as I imagined myself standing inside the scene which Bruegel had painted in 'The Harvesters'. Let's imagine we're there, along with the harvesters working their scythes, or eating together, or asleep under the tree. We're there, and the harvesting is going on all around us. What would it feel like, and what would we see?

The art historians were horrified. 'You are not supposed to do that!' they said. 'You are supposed to be analysing the painting, not putting yourself inside it.' But that's where this idea of the dwelling perspective came from. It developed from there. Particularly in archaeology, however, the notion of taskscape, along with the dwelling perspective, was picked up rather uncritically as a conceptual tool that could be 'used'. It gained a life of its own, in studies of the reconstructed 'taskscape' of this, that and the other prehistoric site. Most of these studies unfortunately missed the point, namely, that the reason for introducing the concept of taskscape was to show how, in the end, we don't need it.

Philip Tonner

You have recently indicated that you might prefer the term 'habitation', to draw out the implications of the position that you have been developing. Adopting this term would mark a departure from the term 'dwelling'. So my question is: what's in a name – dwelling or habitation?

Tim Ingold

The trouble with dwelling lay in its association with the writings of Martin Heidegger, although I actually settled on the term some time before I read Heidegger's famous essay of 1954, 'Building, Dwelling, Thinking'. But, anyway, for many critics, when they see a word like dwelling, an image of Heidegger immediately comes to mind, and with it a plethora of Heideggerian associations. Some of these associations are fine, and some are inspiring, but many are not. The ones that are not are where dwelling gets coupled with the idea of *Lebensraum*, space for living, the space you've cleared out in the forest. To dwell then becomes a very local thing: here you are sitting cosily by the fire in your peasant cottage, surrounded by your fields, with the trees around marking the horizon – an enclosed life space. There are so many problematic things about this, and not only because of the way *Lebensraum* was adopted as a keyword in Nazi propaganda. For my part, I wanted to emphasise that it is precisely *not* by staying in one place that people dwell in the world. They dwell by moving around.

It was partly a strategic choice. I had been using this word 'dwelling', and thought I knew what I meant by it. But others would read all these Heideggerian overtones into it, leading to what I felt was unwarranted criticism. I was being criticised for 'Heideggerisms' that I never intended. To deal with this, I thought, I had better adopt a more neutral word. So I switched to habitation. This turned out to be a profitable move, however, because I soon discovered that the word 'habit', or 'to inhabit', opened up all sorts of new perspectives that I hadn't really thought about before, and which I'm still exploring now. There's a lot of really interesting writing about habit, beyond the reductionist view of it as something you do automatically, without thinking. For me, habit is primarily about the way in which one inhabits a world. The term has connotations of customary use, of dress and of care. It's such a tremendously interesting and productive concept that in retrospect, I'm rather glad to have taken it on board.

Philip Tonner

Given this terminological shift, how should we remain sensitive to what you have described as a 'poetics of dwelling', both in our lives and in our works?

Tim Ingold

What I mean by a 'poetics of dwelling' is that we are perpetually making a world through our activities. We make this world, however, from *within* our involvement in it. That's what 'poetics' says to me. It comes from *poiésis*, making, and tells me that whatever we are making, whether it be artefacts or knowledge, or other people, or history, or all these things, it is carried on from within the world that we inhabit. And this applies to science too. I'm not in principle anti-science, but I do insist that we could do much better science if we could only understand that science itself is a fundamentally poetic endeavour. The problem I see with scientists is that they insistently deny this, at least in their rhetoric and in their public pronouncements. They want to believe that scientific knowledge is completely independent of our habitation of the world, and that it is on precisely this independence (framed as 'objectivity') that its authority rests. This seems to me to be an incoherent position, which weakens science rather than strengthens it. I think our ways of knowing, scientific or not, could be made more honest and ethical, if their poetics was built into them from the start and regarded not as a problem or a weakness, but as a source of strength and indeed power.

Diego Maria Malara

You have equated the perception of the landscape to an act of remembrance, clarifying that remembering is not so much a matter of calling up an internal image stored in the mind, but more a matter of engaging perceptually with an environment that is itself pregnant with the past. How did you come to this realisation and what approaches were you pushing back against?

Tim Ingold

I don't remember exactly what triggered this, but what I do remember is reading a brilliant article, which summed it all up for me. It's by a psychologist called David Rubin. I know nothing about him or about what else he has written, but a short essay of his happened to be included in an edited volume on the psychology of memory, edited by Ulrich Neisser and Eugene Winograd, published in 1988. Rubin's essay was called 'Go for the Skill'. In it he says there are two ways in which you can approach just about anything. One way is what he calls 'a complex structure, simple process model', and the other is a 'complex process, simple structure model'. The 'complex structure, simple process model', which Rubin is criticising in his essay, has long been the dominant one in cognitive psychology. This says that what we have in the mind, in our cognitions, are exceedingly complicated structures, but that the action that follows from these cognitions is entirely straightforward. Speaking of memory, the idea is that to do anything from memory means acting out a structure recalled from the store in your head – a structure already implanted there, perhaps from the previous generation, through some mechanism of transmission.

You could compare this to playing a piece of pre-recorded music. Suppose it has been recorded on vinyl, for an old-fashioned gramophone. It might be a symphony, an exceedingly complicated piece of work, and on the groove of the record it is captured in an incredibly complex line, which the needle follows when the record rotates. However, the mechanism of the record player, which translates the vibration of the needle into an auditory signal, is relatively simple – it's straightforward mechanics. So that would be a 'complex structure, simple process' model. But in the live performance of the symphony by an orchestra, the situation is entirely different. There's an incredibly complicated process, out of which the music emerges, but for which there are relatively few structural prerequisites. The difference between the recorded music on the record player and the actual performance by a symphony orchestra is equivalent to the difference between the two models.

Now, of course, the instrumentalists of the symphony orchestra are remembering how to play the piece, even as they play it. They might even play from memory, but the remembering is done *in* the performance. It's not as if they first go inside their heads to retrieve the structure, and then simply act it out. That was Rubin's point. It is such an elegant contrast, and sums it all up. Out of this comes an idea, which goes back to the psychology of Frederic Bartlett, back in the 1930s, that we should start not with memory, but with *remembering*. Instead of saying there are structures of memory, and that when we remember something, we access the structure, and then write it out; we say there are processes of remembering. This is to say that remembering is itself an environmentally situated and intentional activity, something we do in the world. Whatever we've remembered, or whatever we claim to remember, emerges out of that activity. The music is not pulled out from a storehouse; it's not retrieved ready-made from the attic. It's continually recreated in performance. The act of performance, in giving birth to the music, is itself the act of remembering. It's a way of keeping the thing alive. It's a life process.

That's what I was trying to get at. What I was pushing against, just like Rubin in the essay I mentioned, is the cognitivist approach that always wants to put as much structure as possible into the mind, right from the start. The alternative strategy would be to say, 'Let's see how far we can get by having as little structure in the mind as possible.' If we find we can't do it all, then we'll put a bit of structure in there. But instead of assuming a priori that all the structure is in the mind, let's assume that none of it is, and see how far we can get.

Diego Maria Malara

In 2016, 'The Temporality of the Landscape' was at the centre of a polite, but rather lively debate published in the pages of the *Norwegian Archaeological Review*, and stemming from an extended revisitation of your piece by archaeologist and curator Dan Hicks. If I read your reply correctly, one of the main problems you saw with Hicks's critique is that he sidelines your main arguments. What, in your view, is at stake in this debate?

Tim Ingold

I don't really have any major disagreements with Dan. It's just that he is basically a curator, and he starts from there. He is keen to promote what he calls an 'archival turn'. He is concerned with what we do with objects from the past, and with how practices of archiving and curation can contribute to the growth of archaeological knowledge. I have no problem with this, but it is not what my essay was about. My concern, in writing 'The Temporality of the Landscape', was rather to understand the processes through which the world we inhabit comes into being. Thus, we were really just starting from different ends. If Dan missed the point of what I was trying to do with the essay, it is because he read it from the wrong end. He was already looking at the landscape from his curatorial perspective, and thinking about what archaeologists do when they've excavated a site, when they've interpreted the objects discovered there, and when they're in a position to start telling a story about this landscape and how it was formed. These are all genuine problems, which museum curators routinely face in dealing with their material. But they are not the problems I set out to address in my essay. I wasn't thinking about what archaeologists do with all the stuff they've dug up, how they display things in museums, how they write accounts, reports, records and so forth. I was at the other end, trying to think about what it means to live in a landscape that is always on the point of coming into being.

I guess the lesson of the exchange is that scholars read things differently, and that where they're coming from depends very much on the sorts of practical, day-to-day problems on their minds. I had one set of problems, concerning the temporality of the landscape, Dan had another, concerning the temporality of remains *in* the landscape. This is entirely reasonable and legitimate. His blunder, however – and it *was* a blunder – was to have confused the two.

Philip Tonner

You've written about parallels between growing artefacts and growing children. Interestingly, both involve education. Can you reflect on these parallels in connection with your recent work on education, and can you indicate how you're thinking about growth and related matters in relation to your earlier concept of the taskscape?

Tim Ingold

To start from your last question, the point is that with the taskscape I was thinking about what happens when you take what people are doing in an environment as your point of departure. It's through doing things that people grow and are grown. Suppose you are an anthropologist and you land up in some community, and you ask people when you meet them: 'What are you making?' Alternatively, you could ask: 'What are you doing?' I think you'd probably get different kinds of answers to these two questions. If you ask 'What are you making?', then probably the answer will be 'I'm making a basket' or 'I'm making a pot' or 'I'm making dinner'. The answer will be in terms of some sort of end-product, some objective that the person has in mind at that moment. But if you ask 'What are you doing?', then you will likely get an answer in terms of a task that is still underway. The emphasis is on the process, on the task, not on the object that might be produced through carrying out that task. Naturally, the taskscape leads immediately to the idea of 'doing' rather than 'making', and doing then leads, naturally, to growing things, which is the process: the process by which things come into being, rather than the final end product.

What I've been attempting all the way through, I think, is to reverse the priority of 'making' over 'growing', or 'making' over 'doing'. For me, the 'doing' or 'growing', rather than the 'making', comes first. This reversal is there in the way in which I have been talking about artefacts and children, but it's also at the back of my rethinking of education, where I argue that the point of education is not to produce children in a certain mould, with a certain destiny, and with their potential realised, but rather to make it possible for children to grow – thinking of growth, here, not as a movement from a start point to an end point, but as a movement of continuous birth, of ongoing maturation. It's not a question of one or the other – of choosing between 'making' and 'doing', or between 'building' and 'dwelling'. It's a question of which comes first; to which do we grant ontological priority? Let us give priority to 'doing' and 'growing' over 'making' and 'building'. What then happens if we introduce this reversal of priority into the way we think about education? We're always hearing about students' grades, as if in the end these were all that mattered. Kids are of course pleased to have good grades; it gives them an entry ticket to a career, and all the rest of it. But what has happened to education, when the point of it is simply to come out at the other end with your grades? Is it not also important that your mind was actually expanded along the way, that you could learn things, notice things you didn't notice before? None of that seems to matter once you've got your grades. I believe it is imperative that we get our priorities sorted out, because as things stand at the moment, they are seriously distorted.

Philip Tonner

You have written about a genuinely anthropocentric and spherical, as opposed to a global, approach to environmental thinking. Can you explain what you mean by this and relate it to current developments and debates about environmental sustainability and the global climate crisis?

Tim Ingold

Yes, I have been concerned about the misuse of the term 'anthropocentrism'. I think we've got ourselves into a terrible muddle over this particular concept. Most people who would sign up to the green agenda, as indeed I would, tend to say that we need to get beyond anthropocentrism, which is responsible for so many bad things, for environmental destruction and consequent climate change. By anthropocentrism, they seem to mean a way of thinking which puts humans on top, over and above everything else, as though the planet were simply theirs to possess and exploit for their own ends. Fair enough; this attitude is harmful. Yet these same people – many of them academics – who say we need to get beyond anthropocentrism also argue for a more body-centred approach. We need to recentre our way of life, they say, by putting sensuous, bodily existence at the heart of things.

But how on earth can you say, on the one hand, that we should place the human body and its experience at the centre, and on the other hand, that anthropocentrism is bad? It doesn't make any kind of sense to say that you are overcoming anthropocentrism by placing the human body at the centre of everything. In fact, the view that humans are somehow in possession of the world doesn't put them at the centre of it at all; it puts them either at the apex of a pyramid with the rest of the world at its feet, or outside the world altogether. Humans, in this view, live all around on the outside of the world. From there, they have colonised it and taken possession of it. But that's the very opposite of being at the centre. Literally, it is 'anthropo-circumferentialism'!

It's high time to sort this out. First, we should detoxify the idea of anthropocentrism, so as to enable us to say that putting our human selves at the centre of the world is absolutely right and proper, and moreover ethically necessary if we are to take any kind of responsibility for what goes on in it. How can we claim to be ethically responsible for what is going on in the world, and yet object to anthropocentrism? Then we should find a way of thinking about environmental sustainability which doesn't demonise humans. It doesn't help to blame humans for everything and demand that they should be excluded from the equation; that we should aspire to an environment that is human-free. This would not only be a betrayal of coming human generations; it would also reinforce the very exteriorisation of humans from the environment which caused the problem in the first place. Rather, we need a way of thinking about environmental relations that allows humans to be there, in the midst of things. Only if they're in the midst, able to experience things directly and to develop a sensitivity towards them, can they assume responsibility for what goes on there.

It is the Bezoses and Bransons of this world – these guys who believe that having messed up our own planet, the future lies in taking off into outer space and finding other planets to live on – who are the real culprits. They would rather shoot off from the surface of the earth than stay on the ground and make themselves at home on it.

(B) MATERIALITY

Diego Maria Malara

In your article from 2007, 'Materials against materiality', you suggest that while we speak increasingly about materiality in anthropological circles, our discussions are, paradoxically, becoming more and more abstract and removed from the tangible properties of materials and their concrete affordances. Why do you think that materiality as opposed to materials has become central to anthropological debates? And how do you think these debates should be re-oriented?

Tim Ingold

There are indeed multiple paradoxes here. We have a wealth of literature on the new materialism, much of it expressed in the most obscure, abstract and self-referential of terms, which nevertheless exhorts us to engage with real stuff. If only the materialists would practise what they preach, and get closer to materials themselves, they might write in a language that doesn't consistently shy away from them. But they don't. There's a famous story about Sir James Frazer[1], who, when asked whether he had ever met any of the 'savages' he wrote about at such length, replied: 'Heaven forbid that I should have such misfortune.' It's a bit the same, I think, with many of these theorists of materiality. If you ask them: 'Well, have you ever sawn a plank or done anything else useful with your hands?', they'd say: 'For God's sake, I am a scholar! I work at a laptop, don't put me in front of these crazy materials, I wouldn't know where to start.' You would expect any self-respecting anthropologist to say: 'Well, if we're going to understand materials, it would be a good idea to get our hands dirty and work with them and get to know them, in much the same way as any DIY enthusiast, builder or joiner would do – it would be worthwhile experience from which we could learn.'

I still feel this paradox. It hasn't gone away, for the simple reason that it is intrinsic to academia. Compared with scholars of many other disciplines, anthropologists aren't too bad. We do tend to keep our feet on the ground, for obvious reasons, but if you visit the literature in human geography, or in some areas of philosophy, art history, or science and technology studies, it's completely ridiculous: you can't talk about anything without it being cast as one or another kind of materiality! I have called it the 'concretisation of hyper-abstraction': you start with the concrete stuff and say: 'Right, that's matter'; then you say, 'and matter is material' – and that's a bit more abstract; but then you turn 'material' into an even more abstract noun, 'materiality'. Next thing you know, the different kinds of stuff you started with

---

1 Sir James Frazer (1854–1941), prominent evolutionary anthropologist and folklorist, author of *The Golden Bough* (1890).

reappear as 'multiple materialities'. Instead of wood, you have the materiality of wood; instead of brick, the materiality of brick! This is academic snobbery, pure and simple, dressed up as scholarship. The simple carpenter or bricklayer speaks merely of wood and brick; but look at us: we can speak of the *materiality* of wood and the *materiality* of brick! This is to lift the tenor of our discourse onto an altogether higher intellectual plane. I once asked an archaeologist who was working on mud-brick houses in Ancient Egypt how she would distinguish the materiality of mud from the mud itself. She hadn't a clue!

So let's get back to the stuff itself. In part, this is no more than a protest against scholastic gobbledygook, of which there's a vast amount; trying to make something look deeper, more scholarly, more sophisticated theoretically than it really is by dressing it up in fancy language that turns out to be completely redundant. Behind the words, there's nothing more than what you started with.

That's part of it. But my essay 'Materials against materiality' came out a few years before the new materialism really took off. It is a label that covers all sorts of different approaches, not all of which are compatible with one another. But the one thing these approaches have in common is a commitment to take materials seriously, and that was also the plea at the core of my essay. Until then the study of material culture was focused almost exclusively on objects – on how objects are used and consumed rather than produced or made. Materials were left in the dark. So, there's been a welcome shift of emphasis from objects to materials, and maybe my essay played a small part in bringing this about.

But at the time I wrote it, the problem was that the concept of materiality was being used in a way that reproduced and reinforced the old dichotomy between humanity and nature. The concept of humanity itself had become duplicitous, referring at one moment to humans in the raw, so to speak – that is, as a biological species, on a par with other species in nature – and at the next moment, to a condition of being – the 'human condition' – which was held to lie over and above the natural world. It seemed to me that the same thing had happened to materiality: there was something called 'raw materiality', which is the stuff in itself, and then there was materiality in its other sense, referring to its incorporation into particular human projects. So the term was being used in this duplicitous way: at one moment, for the raw stuff and, at another moment, to its humanisation. And this merely reproduced the division between humanity and nature that I was determined to dissolve.

Diego Maria Malara

Responding to 'Materials against materiality', Christopher Tilley (2007) finds your fundamental distinction between materiality and materials unhelpful. He suggests that we need the concept of materiality in order to account for how brute materials become important for specific groups and social relations. While recognising the importance of your emphasis on properties, Tilley argues that only a limited number of materials and properties become significant to people and acquire social life in relation to them. How would you respond to this objection today? And do you think that your model can account for Tilley's emphasis on social entanglements?

Tim Ingold

This carries on from what I was just saying. The approach which Chris has taken, and with him the entire school of material culture studies centred on University College London,[2] rests on the distinction between 'brute materiality', so called, and the way in which specific materials become important to people or societies in their particular, culturally and historically situated projects. The limitations

---

2 Along with Daniel Miller, Chris Tilley was among the founders of this School, which is represented by its own journal, *Journal of Material Culture*, published since 1996. Sadly, Chris passed away in March 2024, just as this text was in the final stages of editing. For a tribute, see https://www.ucl.ac.uk/social-historical-sciences/news/2024/mar/memory-professor-christopher-tilley.

of the approach, for me, lay in its insensibility towards the life or vitality of materials. A material may have certain properties that make it useful for some purposes but not others; but when you try to pin down what is this stuff, this material, it turns out not to be an object of any kind, but something living, continually moving and transforming, to some extent of its own accord.

Take wool, for example. You might say: 'Wool has certain properties and, if you're going to spin it into yarn, and use the yarn for knitting or weaving, then some properties are more important than others, and we can concentrate on these properties and forget about the others.' But then you ask yourself: 'What about the history of wool? This is stuff that's grown on the backs of sheep, then it's been sheared, it's been cleaned, washed, carded and combed before being eventually spun, even before it gets into the hands of the weaver or knitter, who will then use a variety of instruments and micro-gestures to bind it together in certain ways – unless of course the wool is used to make felt.' If you think about all of that, then what we call wool turns out not to be anything of which you could say, definitively: 'Here it is; this is wool.' It rather turns out to be a story, of growth and transformation, in which whatever properties it may have are ever emergent. Properties are always coming into being and changing and being transformed through the things that are done to the material. Wool has different characteristics on the back of sheep than it does in a piece of felt, or in a woven blanket.

This, I thought, is what is missing from the standard material culture approach, partly because of the latter's greater concentration on consumption than production. It wasn't really looking at how things get made, at what materials do, what their proclivities are, the ways they mutate. If instead you focus on these processes, then the various kinds of treatments become central rather than peripheral. It's a bit like what we were talking about earlier with 'making' and 'growing'. It's saying that we need to focus on the processes first, and to realise that the material is perhaps better understood as a verb rather than as a noun. It's a going on; it's things happening. That's what I was trying to say.

Environment, perception and skill

As ever, it all began with teaching. I had the students in my class sit around the room, in a circle. In the centre was a small table, on which I had placed a stone – a particularly beautiful, rounded stone, which I had collected from the beach near my home in Aberdeen. But before placing the stone there, I had put it under the water tap. It was wet all over. At the start of my class, I told the students to take a good look at the stone. Then, at the end, I asked them to look again. 'It's not the same as when we started, so what has happened?' As soon as you ask this question, all sorts of other questions come up: What is the stoniness of stone? Why does it look so different, now that it's dried out, from when it was wet? What's the relationship between the stone, tapwater and atmospheric air? The students realised that a whole lot of things had been going on, under their very noses but without their paying any attention, even as the class was going on. All of this requires a much more dynamic understanding of materials, which anyone who works with them needs to know. It's part of their competence.

Diego Maria Malara

Tilley essentially claims that in approaching the recursive relation between things and people you tend to ignore the ways in which the experience of materials has profound effects on people's lives and their understanding of the world they live in, as well as of their actions. Thus, he claims that you seem to analyse materials only in terms of themselves. Do you think this aspect of the relation between people and things is neglected in your paper?

Tim Ingold

No, I don't. I am often accused, along these lines, of isolating things from one another and of neglecting the social – neglecting the ways in which things are incorporated or enrolled into human lives. I think this accusation misses the point, which is that I am trying to find another way of talking about how human lives and lives of other kinds are bound up with one another. It's not through some sort of networking, but rather through the ways in which they 'correspond' (that's the word I've used), the ways in which they go along together, answer to one another, and differentiate themselves from one another as they go. If you miss this point, then you can easily misunderstand the argument precisely as Tilley does. He's still partitioning the world between people here and things there, so as to frame material relations as between people and things. He is so stuck in this mindset that he doesn't get the point.

(C) SKILL

Robert Gibb

You've written extensively about skill. What prompted you to start working on this topic? What can anthropology gain from a focus on skills? And what kind of epistemological assumptions should we consider as decidedly outdated?

Tim Ingold

It is hard to say how it all started. I had been thinking about technology – the anthropology of technology – partly because I was teaching a course at Manchester, in ecological anthropology, called 'Environment and Technology'.[3] I felt at the time that existing anthropological approaches to technology were inadequate, in all sorts of ways. There was an assumption that technology wasn't really a matter for anthropologists at all, it was just an external factor, like climate, having nothing directly to do with social relations. If you really wanted to understand technology, then you should talk to engineers and not go asking anthropologists. I felt there was something wrong with this – that technology had become disembedded

---

3   For more on this course, see Conversation 1.

from social relations in a way not dissimilar to what had happened with the economy. Economic anthropology is founded on a critique of the idea that the economy can be cut out from social relations – showing that this idea has its roots in the economic history of the western world – and I was sure the same thing could be said for technology. I wanted to bring technology back into the fold of the social.

In the course of doing this, of considering how we might think of technology as a social practice, I began to worry about the distinction between technology and technique. Surely, I thought, ways of working, which we call techniques, are not to be confused with technology, by which we tend to mean the machines, the tools, the equipment or perhaps a body of formal, objectified knowledge surrounding them. But it also seemed to me that the very idea of technique is a rather narrow refinement of the much more general idea of skill. I suppose I wandered into an approach to skill from that angle: starting from technology and then trying to think how we can re-embed it within a performative and processual understanding of social practice. This re-embedding of the technical with the social was by no means unique to my own endeavours. It was going on more widely in the mid-1980s. Others were thinking along the same lines, most notably Bryan Pfaffenberger.

The question of skill, then, became quite central to my work. The problem was how to define it. And it seemed to me that it had to be defined not in terms of particular technical operations for doing this or that, but as the coordination of perception and action in any given task. On this, I drew inspiration not only from the ecological psychology of James Gibson, to which I have often referred in our earlier conversations, but also from other sources – most notably the pioneering work of the Russian neurophysiologist Nicholai Bernstein, 'On Dexterity and its Development'. With Gibson and Bernstein, I recognised that skill is something that can be trained and educated, and that when we compare differences between people of the kind that we would traditionally have called cultural, what we're really dealing with are differences in skill.

Through your upbringing in a particular cultural environment, you learn to do certain things – you become skilled in certain practices. Learning these skills is learning how to attend to things as you go along, learning how to coordinate perception and action. A clumsy person is someone who lacks the necessary coordination; a skilled person is someone whose perception and action are well coordinated. Once you start thinking about variations of culture in terms of variations of skill, all sorts of possibilities open up. In my case, it enabled me to break down the boundaries between social, psychological and biological dimensions of human existence. In thinking about skill, these all come together as one.

When it comes to obsolete assumptions, the key assumption has to do with the relative priority – again, it is a question of priority, these are not mutually exclusive – of skill and knowledge. The mainstream view, which remains so in educational circles, is that knowledge trumps skill: the knowledge comes first, skill lies merely in its application. You go to school to acquire the knowledge; then you go out into the world to apply it in skilful practice. Skill, in this view, is the application of knowledge already acquired. If you are looking for an epistemological assumption that is definitely outdated, this is it! We need to invert it. This is to argue that there's skill, and there's knowledge, but knowledge emerges out of skill, not the other way around.

Robert Gibb

In your essay 'Of string bags and birds' nests: Skill and the construction of artefacts', you state that 'the study of skill, in my view, not only benefits from, but *demands* an ecological approach'.[4] Please could you explain what you mean by this, and how the approach to understanding skill that you have adopted differs from other perspectives?

---

4 Ingold (2000/2011b: 353, italics in original).

Tim Ingold

It goes back to thinking about skill as the coordination of perception and action. The ecological approach means looking at action and perception as the functioning of a system of relations set up by virtue of the presence of the skilled practitioner in an environment. The alternative would have to lie in a literal application of Marcel Mauss's idea of 'techniques of the body'. Mauss's eponymous essay, dating from 1934, was remarkable in that it was the first to put these issues on the table. But in his view, practitioners embody particular techniques for doing things simply due to their enculturation. People have different techniques of walking, for example, because they've been trained to walk in this way or that, deemed appropriate to their age, gender and social status. This would have nothing to do with the relations between your feet and the ground; it was the way you walk, period. In Mauss's theory the environment doesn't really come into it, except as a setting in which you can apply the cultural knowledge you've received through your training. In an ecological approach, by contrast, the environment enters actively into the formation of the skill; it's not simply a setting in which you apply rules of movement that you've already acquired.

Robert Gibb

From several of the chapters on skill in Part III of *The Perception of the Environment* (notably Chapters 15 and 17), I gained the impression that you have found the work of Karl Marx 'good to think with' (for want of a better expression). Would you agree? And if you do, please could you tell us when you started to read Marx, and how a critical engagement with his work has helped you to develop your own ideas.

Tim Ingold

That's absolutely right! I'm not a Marxist by any means, but the great thing about Marx – particularly the early work – is that he's really thinking: it's tremendously engaging and stimulating to read, and it helps you to work out your own ideas. It doesn't mean you're simply following what he says, as a matter of dogma; it's actually very open-ended writing that invites you in and says: 'Well, look, let's think about this.' So yes, the early works of Marx were definitely good to think with. I can't remember exactly when I started reading them, but it must have been around the early 1980s, when I was teaching a course on anthropological theory at Manchester. This was also a time when neo-Marxism suddenly became *du jour* in anthropology: Maurice Godelier, Emmanuel Terray, Claude Meillassoux, Étienne Balibar and others, many of them influenced by Louis Althusser, were all writing around the same time, and they had quite an impact. There was a brief spurt of writing in neo-Marxist anthropology. It lasted only about five years, and then completely vanished, as suddenly as it had appeared. But for that brief while, it was very prominent and I got caught up in it. There was a great deal of mindless jargon; everybody was trying to figure out what everybody else meant. Some of it was nonsense, but yes, I did find it 'good to think with', and it helped me develop all sorts of ideas.

In many ways, Marx was anthropologically ahead of his time. For example, there's one place in his notebooks from 1857–58 (subsequently published as the *Grundrisse*), in which he discusses the relationship between the individual and society, explaining how what we call the individual can only exist as a social being, can only be constituted as such within the fabric of social relations.[5] How long did it take for anthropology to get beyond the classic Durkheimian dichotomy between the individual and society? Marx was already there, but nobody was reading his work. Then I read Marx, and thought: 'Well, there it is. Perfectly clear.' If you want to understand human slavery, for example, you have to start from this position. Marx asks such big but basic questions: What is a human being? What's the relationship between a human being and the earth? What

---

5   Marx (1973: 265). I discuss this passage at greater length in *Evolution and Social Life* (Ingold 1986a: 256–7).

does labour mean? These are questions I felt were important, and he was already struggling with them.

I even came to the idea of dwelling – although Marx didn't use the term – when I was trying to figure out what we should mean by 'to produce', and how we can get beyond the idea of production as simply producing commodities. 'To produce' means, originally, to bring forth. There's a wonderful passage in a text that Marx co-wrote with Friedrich Engels, *The German Ideology*, in which he explains how producers produce their own and others' material lives: producing is actually living. This, I thought, is to understand 'to produce' as an intransitive verb, not a transitive one. It is not that you are producing this or that; rather, you are *producing*, period; that is to say, you are *living*. And I asked myself, is this not the same as dwelling? *To produce is to dwell*. And that was before I had even read Heidegger! I'd already come to this idea of dwelling because I was thinking of something equivalent to producing your 'actual material life', as Marx and Engels called it. Then I read Heidegger, and realised that this is exactly what he was saying as well.

So in that sense, yes, reading Marx was great. I wish people would go back to reading him, without any kind of preconceptions about Marxism or about the history of communism or about the terrible things that have happened in the world in his name. He was just a very interesting thinker. A bit muddled perhaps, but all the more stimulating because of that!

Robert Gibb

In your essay 'Work, Time and Industry', which appears as Chapter 17 of *The Perception of the Environment*, you distinguish between two different ways of understanding time, activity, production and exchange: the 'dwelling' and 'commodity' perspectives, respectively. You suggest that people subject to 'the temporal dynamic of industrial society' are 'human beings whose lives are caught up in the painful process of negotiation between these extremes'.[6] Please could you tell us what you mean by this.

Tim Ingold

I believe it is wrong to say that modern people live by clock time, whereas pre-industrial, pre-modern people don't – that they simply live by the rhythms of their bodies and of the surrounding world. Since we all inhabit a world, and all have (or rather are) bodies – since we live under the sun, and in a world with seasonal or other variations – the experience of a time linked to natural or bodily rhythms is common to everyone. It's not some sort of romantic myth from pre-industrial times. The particular problem that modern people face is not that they're stuck in one temporal regime rather than another. It is that they have somehow to accommodate their experience of life to a regime that consistently denies it.

This happens again and again. It is very apparent, for example, in health and medicine. People may feel well, sick or whatever, but if something goes wrong, they are forced to confront a medical establishment that continues to regard the body as a kind of chemical machine. Not only patients but doctors as well – if they are any good – have somehow to negotiate between these two things, the experience and the machinery. It's the same for an industrial worker whose labour is being timed by the clock, who has to clock in and clock out. They have somehow to adjust their own inner experience of time to the time of the clock. It's not that they're in clock time, and the pre-industrial person is in body time; it is that, unlike their pre-industrial predecessors, they have to reconcile the two.

I suppose this largely goes back to the constitution of the state, and to its accompanying regime of industry, which at every point seems intent on denying the reality of experience. This is at the heart of the condition we call modernity. That's why I find the

---

6   See Ingold (2000/2011b: 338).

writings of medieval philosophers so fascinating; they are very anthropological in their sensibilities. But since they were writing before modernity began – because it hadn't yet happened – they didn't have to explain their position by reacting against it. They're not caught up in this negotiation, and so their ideas come out very differently.

Robert Gibb

Over the course of the chapters about skill in *The Perception of the Environment*, you seek variously to 'soften' or 'dissolve' distinctions that you claim are peculiar features of Western modernity. In particular, you argue that the dichotomies between biology and culture, on the one hand, and between evolution and history, on the other, can be dispensed with. Why is it important to do this, in your view, and how can we avoid using such dichotomies?

Tim Ingold

It's important, I think, because these dichotomies – particularly the one between biology and culture – are holding us back. As long as we're stuck with them, it seems impossible to move forward. We just go around in circles. There have been endless attempts to show how we can link the biological and the cultural, put them together, reconcile them, integrate them, but we're not actually getting anywhere. Terms like 'biology' and 'culture' are like millstones around our necks, making it impossible to get out of the rut we've been in for many decades. That's why I think it's important to move beyond them. But I admit that to avoid using them altogether is next to impossible. We have to make do with the hand that language has given us, so to speak, otherwise nobody will understand what we're talking about. It's fair enough to say that just as geographers have space and psychologists have mind, anthropologists have culture. It's their thing. For biologists, biology is their thing. It's hard to imagine a future biology that would never use the term 'biology', or a future anthropology that would never use the term 'culture'. We are, to a degree, stuck with the terms we've got.

I think the way to go, where possible, is to treat these terms as questions rather than answers. So we can keep culture as the name of a question: that question is: 'Why do humans do things differently?' But it's not the answer. The answer is inevitably much longer and more complicated. That's what we're doing in anthropology, finding the answer (or answers) to this question. It takes a lot of effort and a lot of thinking and a lot of writing. It can't be summed up in one word. To say that humans do things differently 'because of their culture' is not only circular; it also short-circuits the entirety of what we do.

It's just the same with biology. Biology was originally the name of a subject of study: the study of living organisms. So fine, let's go and study living organisms! A great thing to do. But let's not say that the result of all that study is something called 'biology'. What has happened, I think, is akin to what the philosopher Alfred North Whitehead called 'the fallacy of misplaced concreteness': words that refer, in an abstract and general way, maybe to a field of inquiry, or to an area that we're interested in, are taken to signify entities that have a real, concrete existence in the world, which are then taken to explain everything else that goes on in it. This is the fallacy of explaining this or that behaviour as 'due to biology' or 'due to culture'. It's not so much a matter of abolishing the words, then, as of extricating ourselves from this kind of fallacious thinking. The fallacy is specifically to turn what are vague words to cover a terrain of interest into objects that define how things within that terrain actually behave.

Robert Gibb

You have written that 'The capabilities of action of both human beings and non-human animals are neither innate nor acquired but emergent properties of the total developmental system constituted by the presence of the agent (human or non-human) in its environment'.⁷ How would you account, in these terms, for the development of your own intellectual curiosity and of the way that you read, as a skill comparable to speaking and writing?

Tim Ingold

Of my own thinking and writing, I would say it is always growing and emerging. One feels constantly on the cusp; ideas never stand still. Compare this with its opposite: the view that really gets me angry, and which you often get from evolutionary psychologists, and even occasionally from anthropologists who are into questions of cultural evolution. It is that culture is an inventory of traits inherited as part of a tradition. I say to them: 'You're a scientist, right? And as a scientist, you're saying that human beings live in cultures, and that their ideas are passed on as inherited traits. But are you not a human being as well as a scientist? If what you say about humans, in general, were applied to you too, why on earth should I take anything of what you say seriously? For it could only be an expression of your cultural tradition.' To which the scientist responds by declaring: 'No, I am no ordinary human being. I am a scientist. And that puts me and my enlightened colleagues in a class of our own, above everyone else. Ordinary people can only say what their culture tells them, but we scientists speak the truth.'

This response is ethically unconscionable and politically obnoxious, yet it is one that evolutionary scientists of a neo-Darwinian persuasion come up with time and again. From their point of view, you are either gifted with the power of independent, rational thought or else one of those benighted souls who are stuck in a culture, and whose task in life is simply to reproduce their traits for the next generation. For me, neither position is remotely acceptable. What, then, is the alternative? It is to explain to scientists who would cast us as one or the other, as either scientific colleague or cultural clone, 'No, actually we are living people who create ourselves and others

---

7   See Ingold (2000/2011b: 366).

through our own ongoing activities in the world, which include imagining, thinking and writing; that's what we're doing.' This is equally true of those who call themselves scientists or scholars as it is of reindeer herders, fishers, farmers or factory workers. We don't have to discriminate along the lines of a divide between reason and culture; indeed, it is quite abhorrent to do so.

That's why it is time to move on from the innate versus acquired dichotomy. By doing so, it becomes possible to understand how what we think and write, our forms of curiosity, can have their own integrity, while also admitting that this integrity is not just given but has to develop, to be worked at, and is always subject to modification, growth or revision. But this also implies that curiosity can be cultivated rather than shut down. And that's what we should be doing as teachers. Some people are more curious than others, but I don't think there is anything innate about this. Curiosity and care go together – they are intrinsic to the ways we are in the world – but there are ways of allowing this curiosity to flourish and there are ways of shutting it down. The worst of so much modern education is that it is deliberately shutting down curiosity, while pretending otherwise, and that's terrible.

Robert Gibb

In reading and writing about skill, your own curiosity has led you to range widely in time and space and across intellectual fields and disciplines.

Tim Ingold

Well, you follow your nose; that's what one does. One thing leads to another. I've found that enjoyable. It's fun, because you're always learning new things.

Further Reading

Ingold first introduced his idea of the 'the mycelial person' in a conference on 'Nature Knowledge', held in Venice in December 1997, but it did not appear in print until eight years later (Ingold 2005b). On the comparable idea of the rhizome, see the first, introductory chapter of Deleuze and Guattari, *A Thousand Plateaus* (2004, first published in 1980).

Influential works on the anthropology and archaeology of landscape, dating from the early 1990s, include Bender (1993), Tilley (1994) and Hirsch and O'Hanlon (1995). Ingold's article, 'The Temporality of Landscape', was published in *World Archaeology* in 1993. Hicks's critique was published as 'The Temporality of the Landscape Revisited' in Volume 49 (1) of *Norwegian Archaeological Review* in 2016. A response by Ingold, 'Archaeology with Its Back to the World' (2016), appeared in the same issue of the journal. In 2017 Ingold himself published a retrospective review of the concept of taskscape, 'Taking taskscape to task' (Ingold 2017b), in a volume marking two decades of taskscapes in archaeology (Rajala and Mills 2017).

Heidegger's essay Building, Dwelling, Thinking was first published in 1954 and is reprinted in *Poetry, Language, Thought* (2013). Rubin's essay, 'Go for the skill', is included in the collection edited by Neisser and Winograd, *Remembering Reconsidered* (1988). Bartlett's classic study, *Remembering*, was first published in 1932 (Bartlett 1992).

Ingold's 2007 article 'Materials against materiality' and Tilley's response 'Materiality in materials' both appear in Volume 14 (1) of the journal *Archaeological Dialogues*. On the re-embedding of the technical with the social, Ingold refers to the anthropological work of Pfaffenberger (1988, 1992). On the question of skill, he refers to Gibson's *The Ecological Approach to Visual Perception* (1979) and to Bernstein's essay, 'On Dexterity and its Development' (1996). Bernstein's work dates from the 1940s but remained unpublished until 1991 (in Russian) and 1996 (in English translation). Mauss's classic essay on 'Techniques of the body' was first published in French in 1934. An English translation appeared in Volume 2(1) of *Economy and Society* (1973).

See Conversation 1 for Ingold's introduction to anthropological neo-Marxism, and relevant references. The two principal sources for Marx's early writings to which Ingold refers here are the notebooks from 1857–8, and *The German Ideology*, co-authored with his collaborator, Friedrich Engels in 1845–6. Neither was published during Marx's lifetime. The notebooks, which had become lost under unknown circumstances, were finally published in a German edition in 1953, and in English, under the title *Grundrisse*, twenty years later (Marx 1973). Part One of *The German Ideology*, with selections from Parts Two and Three, was first published, in English, in 1970 (Marx and Engels 1977).

The philosopher Alfred North Whithead introduced and explained what he calls 'the fallacy of misplaced concreteness' in his Lowell Lectures of 1925, *Science and the Modern World* (Whitehead 1926). Finally, *Why Medieval Philosophy Matters*, by Stephen Boulter (2019), will introduce readers to the relevance of this rich period of the history of philosophy.

CONVERSATION 4:

Animals, lines and imagination

Summary: An interest in human–animal relations has been a feature of Ingold's work from *The Skolt Lapps Today* (1976) to *Imagining for Real: Essays on Creation, Attention and Correspondence* (2022). In the first part of this conversation, Ingold reflects on the development of his thinking about this issue, and explains what he means when he argues for an 'anthropology beyond humanity' (2013). This is followed by a discussion of arguably one of Ingold's most original works: *Lines* (2007/2016). Ingold explains why he thinks we should care about lines, and what the important difference is, in his view, between 'threads' and 'traces'. He then outlines what he means by 'correspondence', a notion that has come to occupy a prominent place in his recent work. The final section is devoted to a discussion of some of the key themes in Ingold's most recent collection of essays, *Imagining for Real*. Ingold explains how, by prioritising 'creation' over 'creativity', he has tried to move beyond the distinction between imagination and reality, before reflecting on his call for a 'one world anthropology' and on some of the challenges facing the discipline's further development. The interview took place on 13 May 2022.

(A) HUMAN–ANIMAL RELATIONS

Robert Gibb

An interest in human–animal relations is a feature of your work from *The Skolt Lapps Today*, published in 1976, through various other publications, to the chapter 'Animals are Us: on Living with Other Beings', in your book *Imagining for Real*, published in 2022. How have your ideas about the relationships between humans and animals, and the human and nonhuman in general, developed over time, and what are some of the key influences that have shaped your thinking on this topic?

Tim Ingold

I first became interested in human–animal relations because I was working with people who, besides hunting, trapping and fishing, were also herding reindeer. Thus, I was writing about relations between humans and reindeer even for my doctoral thesis, and this became the topic of one of my first published articles, 'On reindeer and men', dating from 1974. My interest in the different ways humans relate to reindeer (or caribou, as the same species is known in North America) then grew into a wider, comparative exploration of hunting, pastoralism and ranching as reindeer-based economies in the circumpolar North. That's the context in which I started thinking about these things. I was initially thinking within a fairly conventional framework, namely, that social relations are basically human relations, and that nonhuman animals are part of the natural world. I was interested in the relationship between social and ecological systems, so the assumption was that social relations are confined to the human domain, whereas ecologically, we have to look at the relationship between human and animal populations. That was how I structured it.

And that's indeed how I was thinking when I was writing my book on hunters, pastoralists and ranchers. I did allow that certain animals could be included within the fold of human relations, but only as quasi-humans themselves, through having been socialised into the human group. These were tame animals. But relations of herding, I argued, were more ecological than social, and to study them one had to explore the dynamics of human and animal populations. My ideas began to shift during the 1980s, partly because I had been asked to convene a thematic series of sessions in the World Archaeological Congress of 1986, on cultural attitudes to animals. The full title of the theme – the brainchild of archaeologist and congress convenor Peter Ucko – was 'Cultural Attitudes to Animals, Including Birds, Fish and Insects'. The title was deliberately provocative in its inclusion of animal species of every conceivable kind, and not just the larger, more charismatic creatures which tend first to come to mind when we in the West think 'animal'. And it forced me to examine this question of how we understand animals rather more carefully, especially as I came to write my chapter for the book that later became *What is an Animal?*

One major influence was the work of the philosopher Mary Midgley. She was a redoubtable, fairly elderly lady at that time, who in her later years produced an enormous body of work, specifically on the question of animals. Her books *Beast and Man* and *Animals and Why They Matter*, dating respectively from 1978 and 1983, were hugely influential. Her argument, with which I found myself largely in agreement, was that we shouldn't reserve the study of animals for the natural sciences alone. She didn't dispute the boundary between the humanities and the natural sciences, or that the humanistic understanding of how social life is carried on has to deal with questions of subjectivity, morality and ethics. Her argument, however, was that you could just as well study animals humanistically as study humans scientifically. So, while she accepts the boundary between the humanities and the natural sciences on the one hand, and between humans and animals on the other, for her these boundaries don't align but cross-cut, so as to yield four quadrants: the humanistic study of humans, the humanistic study of animals, the natural scientific study of humans and the natural scientific study of animals. And with the second quadrant, animals are admitted into the field of discussions about morality, ethics, subjectivity and so on.

I was very influenced by this, but I was also getting into the literature on hunting and gathering societies. I had started off working with what were supposed to be a pastoral people, the Sámi, only to discover that for the most part, the animals weren't really being herded at all, but rather roamed free 'in the wild'. I wasn't sure if they were being herded or hunted, and this is what got me into discussions around hunting. I found that anthropologists engaged in hunter-gatherer studies were much more invested in big questions like 'What is the difference between human society and animal society?' and 'How should we understand relations between humans and animals?' Anthropologists working on pastoralism, by contrast, were preoccupied with issues to do with development, and with transitions between nomadism and sedentism. I was more interested in the fundamental, philosophical questions. But I was equally fascinated by the many anthropological studies, particularly of northern Indigenous people, exploring relationships between human beings and the animals they would hunt. This literature described how hunters think of prey species as having societies of their own, and of the hunt itself as a social transaction, in the nature of a gift or sacrifice. A landmark in all of this was a classic study by A. Irving Hallowell, entitled 'Ojibwa Ontology, Behavior and World View', first published in 1960. Not only was this article incredibly prescient, it was also marked out by the way Hallowell would treat his Ojibwa interlocutors as philosophical equals. At least so far as they are concerned, as he showed, social relations are in no wise confined to humans; rather the animals they hunt are equally part of the social field. This was a revelation for me.

So then – by the end of the 80s, and going into the 90s – I came to the conclusion that the division between what I had seen as two distinct domains, respectively of social and ecological relations, was no longer sustainable. We would therefore have to rethink even the human–animal relations of pastoralism, so as to understand them not as ecological relations between human and animal populations, but as social relations of a particular kind. The question was: 'What is particular to the kinds of social relations between humans and animals we characterise as hunting, and how do they differ from the social relations we characterise as herding?' This question led to my 1994 article, 'From trust to domination'. The relationship between the pastoralist and the animals of his herd is indeed a social one, I argued, but it's based on a relationship of domination, rather than on one of trust. But both trust and domination are essentially social relations. Only with modern commercial agriculture does the world of nature come to be so objectified as to reduce animals to mere commodities. This essay on trust and domination was, however, the last serious thing I would write on human–animal relations for a long while. For in the years that followed, I became disillusioned with the whole topic.

What happened was that cultural theorists waded in, coming mostly from literary studies. The majority of these theorists had no practical experience of animals whatever, beyond the family pet, but all of a sudden, human–animal relationships had become the topic *du jour*, and these fashion-following scholars began churning out reams of pretentious literature which completely ignored all the work that we in anthropology, not to mention our colleagues in archaeology, had been beavering away at for years. And I thought, 'I've had enough of this, I'm going to do something else.' When I did eventually return to the theme, in my 2013 article 'Anthropology Beyond Humanity' (first presented as a Westermarck Memorial Lecture at the University of Helsinki), it was to deliver a kind of grumpy-old-man protest, partly directed against the fashionistas of 'multi-species ethnography' and the 'more-than-human', for having wilfully overlooked generations of careful anthropological and archaeological work on human–animal relations.

The fashion for more-than-human studies, I believe, is largely founded on a myth, namely, that it does away with an entrenched division between humans and nonhumans which, until then, had persisted more or less unchallenged. According to this myth, on which many students today are brought up, the social sciences have always taken for granted the absolute dichotomy between humans and animals, and have only recently begun to dismantle it. This is entirely wrong. To see why, you have only to read Lewis Henry

Morgan's classic study of the American beaver, first published in 1868 and still regarded as authoritative today, in which he likens the animal to a human engineer. And it wasn't only Morgan. In fact, you find lots of interesting observations about human–animal relations in the writings of the founding fathers of anthropology and sociology. Both Karl Marx and Max Weber deliberated at length on the theme. From the late nineteenth century and through the first half of the twentieth, scholars of the social sciences, including sociology, were quite open-minded about the human–animal distinction. They would certainly not have put their foot down and insisted that it was absolute. I think the idea of an absolute division came later, around the 1930s, perhaps with the functionalist sociology of Talcott Parsons. From then on, the division became ever more firmly entrenched, but it's a myth to pretend it was always there.

One other figure I should mention, whose work was a revelation to me, is Jakob von Uexküll – Estonian aristocrat, theoretical biologist and retrospectively acknowledged as the founding father of the field now known as biosemiotics. Von Uexküll was writing in the 1930s, but his work was long ignored, and it wasn't until the late 1980s that I first came across it, just at the time when I was trying to figure out what it means to say of humans or other animals that they inhabit an environment. I was equally convinced at the time of two things: first, that humans are uniquely endowed with a capacity for symbolic thought; but second, that not only humans but also other animals inhabit meaningful environments. The question, then, was: 'How can meaning be constituted, for an animal, in the absence of symbolism. What kind of environmental meaning can be non-symbolic?' Von Uexküll offered an answer, through his concept of Umwelt, understood as an environment of signs, but not of symbols. The Umwelt is the environment coloured by the sensorimotor capacities of the animal whose environment it is. Recently, this idea has been revisited in the work of anthropologist Eduardo Kohn, dating from 2013. It has suddenly become very fashionable. But if I may don my grumpy-old-man hat yet again, I was already on to this four decades ago. No-one noticed then!

Diego Maria Malara

At the start of your introduction to the 1988 edited collection *What Is an Animal?*, you raised an important question. To quote you: 'How can we reach a comparative understanding of human, cultural attitudes towards animals, if the very conception of what an animal might be and, by implication, of what it means to be human, is itself culturally relative?' Could you summarise the answer you gave in that seminal book, and explain how it would differ if you were to answer it today?

Tim Ingold

It all comes down to language. At the time I was convinced that language is a uniquely human faculty. I went along with the idea, popularised by Noam Chomsky, that language is essentially a human thing that allows us to reason symbolically – that it isn't just a means of communication, but a means to think, to exercise our faculty of intellect. But I was also convinced that nonhuman animals are conscious, intentional beings. It's just that they don't reflect through language upon their existence in the world, as humans do. At the same time, I was reading the work of philosopher John Searle, on the question of intentionality. It is important, Searle argued, to distinguish between what he called 'prior intentions' and 'intention in action'. We do all sorts of things intentionally, consciously, purposefully, without necessarily having a premeditated plan of what we're trying to achieve. The intentionality that infuses the action itself, Searle argued, must therefore be distinguished from any plan or representation we may have of it.

I linked this distinction to one that was being proposed, around much the same time, by the sociologist Anthony Giddens, between 'practical' and 'discursive' consciousness. Practical consciousness is what it says on the tin: it is the consciousness that infuses what we do 'on purpose'. But discursive consciousness emerges only in our representations or reflections, in words or equivalent media, on what we do. My argument was that humans are unique in their discursive consciousness, and hence in setting up prior intentions. But this doesn't mean that animals lack consciousness, or that they're not intentional beings; it's just that, for animals as indeed for humans much of the time, intentionality is in the action rather than prior to it and the corresponding consciousness is practical rather than discursive. I thought that by making these distinctions we could find common ground, as it were, between humans and animals, and then examine how our specific form of cultural reflexivity can emerge from this ground. That was the answer: that we can have a comparative understanding of attitudes to animals, but only if that understanding is grounded in a sense of the continuity between animals and humans.

I still think that cultural attitudes *towards* animals are a sort of spin-off from our fundamental being-in-the-world *with* animals. I believe it was Michael Jackson who said that we can share an experience of being in the world, but that different people may render it in different ways, according to their own cultural bent. Some talk about it in this way, some talk about it that way, but the grounding in shared experience is what makes cross-cultural communication possible in the first place. I still believe this kind of grounding is the condition for comparative anthropology, but I wouldn't any longer go back to Searle, nor would I want to couch the question in terms of intentionality. That's too cognitive for me, nowadays. My present position is rather that we should understand every animal in terms of what it does: every animal is not just a living thing; it is also a *way of being alive*. And by the same token, I no longer accept the essentialist idea of language as an exclusively human faculty. For me, now, language itself is a process, it's a conversation, it's going on or 'languaging'. It is not some special cognitive faculty that humans carry in their heads. In this regard, I have completely shifted my position from what I held before.

Diego Maria Malara

Could I ask you to clarify what you were saying about language as a 'conversation', rather than an embedded faculty in the head of individuals? Could you give a concrete example?

Tim Ingold

My objection is to the essentialisation of language – to the idea that it's a particular thing or a structure located in the mind. What exist in the world are people moving around, talking, gesticulating, singing, telling stories, doing all that they do. Whether we can draw any clear-cut boundaries between what humans do and what other creatures do is a moot point. It is so contentious that I'm not sure I could even take a stand on it. But instead of regarding language as a structure, I would now regard 'languaging' as something we do. This languaging is not, in the first place, a means of communicating information, but rather the way we humans have of making our presence felt. A dog says 'Here I am' by barking, but a human does it by talking. It's through the voice that we establish our presence in the world. Perhaps because of the structure of the vocal cords, this form of presence may be peculiar to human beings. Other creatures do it differently. But the shift is from thinking about language as a cognitive structure, or a facility to assemble smaller units of cognition into larger ones (like words into sentences), to thinking about language primarily in terms of voice, as a performative modality through which we present ourselves to others.

Diego Maria Malara

Your research has paid particular attention to the process of domestication, using this theme to call into question the universality of Western assumptions about the boundary between the wild and the cultural. Could you briefly outline your main argument about domestication and reflect on the differences between your line of inquiry and the direction that human–animal studies have taken recently?

Tim Ingold

Let me start by going back to what I said about this in my book *Hunters, Pastoralists and Ranchers*, dating from 1980. I wanted to break down the category of domestication into different dimensions. The words I used were taming, herding and breeding. The argument was that taming is a social relation, herding an ecological relation and breeding a technical relation. Since these can occur independently of one another, we have to deconstruct the idea of domestication, which lumps them all together. In those days, I was thinking of taming as what happens when you introduce a living animal into your domestic group, as a member of the household. That's domestication in the most literal sense, since the animal belongs to the *domus*, the house, and is treated accordingly. The animal becomes a quasi-human member of the domestic group. Herding, I thought, is not so personal, since it doesn't require you to know every animal individually. It's more of a contractual relationship, involving protection in exchange for food, between a human population and an animal population. Breeding is simply a technique of selection, which may or may not be carried out deliberately. I wanted to separate these three dimensions.

But that was then. At the time, I still assumed a hard-and-fast division between the sphere of social relations and the sphere of ecological relations. Only with taming, I thought, when animals enter into the human group as quasi-humans, do they cross the boundary between nature and society. Apart from that, human–animal relations are ecological, not social. But once I came to question the division between social and ecological relations, I had to rethink domestication as well. That's when the distinction between trust and domination entered the equation. It is not, I thought, that the relations of the pastoralist to the animals of his herd are ecological rather than social, but rather that they're based on a certain principle of sociality. This is the principle of domination, which I compared to human slavery – which is also a social relation, and not an ecological one. The hunter, by contrast, relates to his prey on the basis of a principle of trust, which, in hunter-gatherer communities, is fundamental to relations among humans as well.

Quite a few colleagues have gone on to critique this 'trust to domination' argument on the perfectly reasonable grounds that in real life, things are more complicated. They point out that trust and domination are not mutually exclusive, and that in most kinds of human–animal relations you find an element of both. Still, the grumpy old man in me sometimes sees anthropology going around in circles, with a new generation declaring that we have to rethink the concept of domestication, apparently unaware of the fact that I was doing this decades ago, as were generations before mine. These sorts of issues come and go with changes of fashion. Domestication was long out of fashion, but is now back in again. Looking over human–animal studies at the present moment, however, there seem to be rather few dealing specifically with pastoral societies. What's new about contemporary studies is that they are dealing with all sorts of other contexts of human–animal encounters, under less traditional circumstances and with a much broader sense of what an animal can be, including, for example, malaria-carrying mosquitoes or soil-transforming earthworms. So the field is changing. But the basic issues, I think, remain much the same.

Robert Gibb

In your 2013 lecture, which you have revised and included in *Imagining for Real*, you argued for an anthropology *beyond* humanity. Please can you explain what you mean by this? In what ways do you think your argument is similar to, or differs from, calls for a multi-species ethnography or an anthropology beyond the human?

Tim Ingold

This relates to the question of the posthuman, or what we understand by posthumanism. What I mean by an anthropology beyond humanity is one that is not defined in terms of the opposition between animality and humanity of the kind that we've inherited from the Enlightenment. I'm not, however, looking for a posthumanism that is *opposed* to humanism, but rather one that will go beyond it. I want to find another way of imagining the human that does not set up the human condition in direct opposition to whatever the nonhuman condition might be. So by 'an anthropology beyond humanity' I don't mean anthropology *after the human*; I want to stay with the human, but I want to move beyond 'humanity' as it came to be defined in the Enlightenment, as a condition that places humans on another level, apart from the rest of creation. That's why I've been particularly attracted to the idea of 'humaning', where 'to human' is a verb, and 'humaning' is what we do. Humanness, if you will, is not given or defined in advance; it is rather a task that we have continually to work at and for which we bear a collective responsibility. It is something we perform. As such, 'humaning' is an ongoing project. It has no conclusion, and it's not progressive; but it carries on. This, then, is what I mean by an anthropology beyond humanity. If anthropology is a speculative inquiry into the conditions and possibilities of human life, then an anthropology beyond humanity is one that would look for this in the ways we can 'human' in the world, rather than trying to specify the conditions that set humanity apart.

I don't much like the term multi-species ethnography, and am tired of the fashion for it. That's for two reasons: one, which we've already discussed (in Conversation 2), has to do with my reservations about ethnography; the other is that I think if we're going to understand living beings as undergoing continuous formation in and through their relations with others, then this is simply incompatible with the species concept – at least in the taxonomic sense that is conventional in modern biology. This concept assumes that your membership of this or that species is given from the start and unalterable. It already imposes a classification onto the world and puts every living being within it. My view is that if we are to move beyond humanity in its Enlightenment sense, then we also have to move beyond the taxonomic idea of the species. We can't simply reproduce it.

So, when it comes to multi-species ethnography, I find myself both for and against. I am *against* both 'multi-species' and 'ethnography', but nevertheless *for* an anthropology that is not confined to the human. This is not, however, such a new idea as its advocates make out – in fact, we've been doing it in anthropology for generations. There is a further risk, exemplified in the work of Kohn, to which I've already referred, of dissolving the boundary between the human and the nonhuman, only to erect a still more unassailable boundary between the world of life and the world of non-life. To suggest that the former is ruled by signs, and the latter only by material and energetic exchange, is, I think, a big mistake. I'm very sceptical of a semiotic approach that would divorce the world of meanings from the world of matter. I think it's a bad move. That's why I eventually came out against the semiotic approach which so attracted me back in the late 1980s, when I was reading von Uexküll. Anyway, that's where I am.

(B) LINES AND CORRESPONDENCES

Diego Maria Malara

Lines represents one of your most original works. I remember reading the book when I was a PhD student and thinking that it takes a very different approach from those studies on similar topics that I had encountered before. Why should anthropologists care about *Lines*? Why do you think that an explicitly anthropological focus on this topic has been somewhat rare?

Tim Ingold

I am as puzzled by your second question as you are. As a book, *Lines* almost wrote itself. It started off as a series of lectures, delivered to an archaeological audience and tailored towards their interests. It has nevertheless appealed to people from all sorts of disciplines and, for me, this has been especially gratifying. Yet it seems that the last discipline to have any interest in the book is my own, namely anthropology. I have long wondered why this should be so. The book seems to be on a different wavelength from that of most contemporary anthropology. One or two sympathetic colleagues have suggested that the problem may lie in my rather antiquated way of using ethnographic examples. Maybe that's part of the problem – that it is not based on one coherent ethnographic study of some people somewhere, which is what you're supposed to do these days. What you are *not* supposed to do is pick up snippets from here, there and everywhere, in the fashion of a Marcel Mauss or a James Frazer.

That might be it. Many anthropologists, not unreasonably, are still hung up about power and coloniality and, if you don't explicitly address these issues or take them as your point of departure, then they don't know how to situate your work. I suppose too, that the book doesn't engage explicitly with the main areas of theoretical debate in the subject at the moment. Perhaps it is what you might call 'left field'. But even if it is somehow off the pitch and hard to place, I still find that, when you mention lines or linearity to anthropologists, the bells it rings are things like linear time, linear causation, linear models of progress, lines of colonisation. At the very beginning of the book, I try to explain that this is just one kind of line. There are many other kinds of lines, which should not be left out. But this is still a barrier for many anthropologists to overcome. They're so stuck with the idea that linearity is the defining feature of Western modernity, imperialism, colonialism, temporality, progress, science and all the rest of it that it takes a while for the point to sink in, that lines can be such generative things.

I'm not sure. I am still puzzled, but I think that's what it is with anthropological readers of *Lines*. They tend to respond that while it is all very interesting, they just don't know what to do with it.

Diego Maria Malara

This is certainly interesting. Why do *you* think anthropologists should care about lines?

Tim Ingold

Because anthropologists are supposed to be interested in human practices, and there is scarcely a human practice that does not involve making a line of one kind or another: speech, writing, walking, weaving, doing anything that involves movement, gesture and rhythm. All of these are linear phenomena.

One of my main sources of inspiration in writing *Lines* was the work of the French prehistorian André Leroi-Gourhan. His magnum opus was entitled *Le geste et la parole* ('Gesture and Speech'). The book, first published in 1964–5, offered an all-embracing synthesis of human evolution and prehistory, in which everything revolves around the themes of technics and language, memory and rhythms. And look what happened! Everyone still canonises Lévi-Strauss. Yet Leroi-Gourhan, his contemporary, has been so completely forgotten that his work was not even translated into English until the 1990s. It's true that it is more widely acknowledged in France, where many regard both scholars, Lévi-Strauss and Leroi-Gourhan, as of equivalent stature. This is in part due to Leroi-Gourhan's special interest in craftsmanship and techniques, drawn from his time spent in Japan. Indeed, Leroi-Gourhan laid the foundations for the anthropological study of techniques, which has remained strong in France but never really took root in the Anglophone world. To be sure, *Gesture and Speech* is a wild book, occasionally crazy, sometimes visionary, often contradictory. But it is packed with ideas, many of them way ahead of their time. And many of these ideas found their way into *Lines*.

Diego Maria Malara

In that book on lines, you make an important distinction between thread and trace, just to clarify soon after that this distinction is not an absolute one, and that these two types of line regularly morph into each other. Could you give us some ethnographic examples of threads and traces, as well as of the dynamics of their transformation?

Tim Ingold

I could recapitulate the ones I give in the book, starting with the thread. I include some discussion of how people in many societies talk about life and death, and about how the dead weave threads in the underworld. There is of course the famous Cretan myth of Ariadne's thread, which was a lifeline for the hero Theseus. But I also cite an example from the Chukchi of northeastern Siberia, who believe that when you die you go to the underworld, where, at least for a while, you are destined to wander through thread-like underground channels or fissures. There is thus a clear distinction between the paths that people inscribe in the surface of the land during their life – these are traces – and the threads they wind as they move around underground after they've died. At the moment of death, traces are converted into threads. You move from the path into the labyrinth. The only people who can return and report on the experience are shamans, who can go back and forth between the two domains. That was one of my examples.

The argument is that traces are turned into threads in the dissolution of surfaces. When you die the surface of the earth dissolves, and you find yourself in a world of threads. So that was about the surface of the earth.

I drew another example from the Abelam people of Papua New Guinea, where the comparison is between making string bags out of fibres and decorating the fronts of their houses with lines. The names they give to these lines are the same as the names they give to the threads of the string bag. Effectively, when you decorate the front of your house with lines you dissolve its surface, turning it into a weave of threads, as in the bag.

My third example was of the Kolam designs, which people in parts of South India place before the entrances to their houses. The tangled lines of the design are supposed to protect the house against invasion by demonic spirits. Again, the argument is that spirits, when they encounter these designs, no longer perceive the door of the house as a surface but get tangled up in the lines, so they never actually get through. These are some examples.

In the other direction, from threads to traces, I concentrate on weaving, knotting and embroidery. Weaving and knitting are the most obvious examples, where you start with a hank of wool, which is one very long line, and through the weaving or knitting you form a surface which has a pattern in it. So the lines you see on the surface are the lines of the pattern rather than the thread-lines themselves. In that case the thread has turned into a trace. Thus, threads turn to traces in the formation of surfaces; traces turn to threads in their dissolution. I can think of lots of other examples, and keep coming across new ones.

Diego Maria Malara

You propose that a history of writing ought to be encompassed within a more inclusive history of notation. I'm sympathetic to this claim, but I have two distinct questions. First, why do you think that this kind of more generous perspective is necessary? And secondly, I'm interested in a rather minor tradition of anthropological research exploring writing and reading which sometimes goes under the label of the anthropology of literacy. How does your intellectual project differ from that kind of tradition?

Tim Ingold

I think these two questions are connected. The answer to the first question of why we need a more generous perspective is that otherwise we're in danger of falling for what is often called the retrospective fallacy – namely, of retrojecting into the past distinctions or categorisations that have only emerged in the course of the very history we're trying to explain. That would be circular. If, for example, you focus on the distinction between writing and drawing, or between writing and musical notation – but let's just take writing and drawing for now – for many of us today it's an obvious distinction, although it isn't in practice as obvious as you might think. But in fact, this particular distinction emerged historically, in quite a complicated story which began with alphabetical writing and ended with the technology of print, perhaps even with computing. The ways in which writing and drawing, or text and image, have separated out have evolved along with that history. We cannot then throw back the outcome of this process – the distinction between writing and drawing as we understand it today – as the framework within which that history is to be understood. We have to come up with a way of defining our area of interest which doesn't presuppose precisely the emergence of that which we want to explain.

I mentioned Leroi-Gourhan a moment ago, and one of his great ideas was that if we're talking about prehistoric people and analysing their engravings, whether on rock or other material, then we cannot prejudge them to be either writing or drawing. All we can say is that they are inscriptions of some kind. He decided to bring all such inscriptions under the label of 'graphism', on the grounds that they are indeed inscriptions and have clearly been made by hand, often with a tool. That, however, is all we can say about them for sure. Only then can we begin to figure them out, interpret them, explain them, speculate on who made them and why. I found this idea of graphism, as a place from which to understand inscriptive practices of all kinds, very powerful. What Leroi-Gourhan proposed, then, was an inclusive history not of writing or of drawing, but of graphism.

In proposing an inclusive history of notation, I had much the same idea in mind, and have Leroi-Gourhan to thank for it. I came to notation because what I was really interested in, to begin with, was how we have come to distinguish in the way we do today between musical notation and writing. I found that in other societies, as in Japan, distinctions have been drawn in a quite different way. We therefore need a way of thinking about this that is more inclusive. I think this answers your second question as well, in a way. The anthropology of literacy is largely concerned with how people, in this present day and age, or at least relatively recent times, have managed to navigate the social and political systems in which they live – systems in which there are schools and bureaucracies, in which power is invested in certain kinds of inscription or documentation. The field of the anthropology of literacy, as I understand it, is addressing these very real issues that people face in recent or contemporary societies, in coping with institutional structures often framed in terms of various forms of literacy.

That's an entirely reasonable thing to do, but my interests were, in a sense, more evolutionary. With Leroi-Gourhan, I wanted to envisage a prehistory and a history in which we could place human practices of all sorts, in their evolutionary emergence. Rather than starting with the world we've got, with all these institutions that people have to cope with, we can go back to the beginning and ask, 'How did all this evolve?' I think that's the difference. I'm still thinking in these broad, rather evolutionary terms of a movement through from prehistory into history. And this of course means that I'm not so focused on the very real problems that ordinary people face in our contemporary world.

Diego Maria Malara

I think the next question is a hybrid one, to which both Philip and I contributed. Philip, would you like to ask it?

Philip Tonner

Thank you, Diego. Tim, in your books on lines, *Lines: A Brief History* and *The Life of Lines*, two sentences stand out to us. The first, from the introduction to *Lines*, is 'Life is lived . . . along paths, not just in places.' To me, this brief statement encapsulates an important part of your argument. It is clearly reminiscent of your earlier work on landscape and movement. I wonder what *Lines* adds to your earlier theorising on these issues? The second sentence, from *The Life of Lines*, is 'To lead a life is to *lay down a line*.'[1] Can you expand on what you mean by this?

Tim Ingold

Thanks. I think these are really two versions of the same question. I had already reached the idea, in *The Perception of the Environment*, that when we speak of a way of life, we have to think of it not as a fixed body of tradition, passed down from one generation to the next, but as a path of movement through the world – a path that you not only actively follow but also improvise as you go along. Hence the focus on lifelines.

It is hardly a new idea to think of ways of life as lifelines. However, once I had begun to imagine lives as movements along ways of life, I kept finding resonances in ethnographic accounts from around the world, even though their significance was not necessarily picked up by the ethnographers themselves. They were simply there in what they reported. For example, I was reading James Weiner's book *The*

---

1   Ingold (2007a: 2; 2015: 118, original emphasis).

Empty Place, on the Foi of Papua New Guinea, in which he describes how people are always making paths through the rainforest, and how these paths, too, have lives. If they're not trodden repeatedly, they soon grow over. I was also reading Claudio Aporta on the way Inuit people find their way around in the Arctic landscape: they say their paths of movement don't go from A to B; they are rather paths along which life is lived, children are born, disputes happen, animals are hunted and so on and so forth. Then I was reading ethnography on the Batek, who are hunter-gatherers of Penang in Malaysia, in which the ethnographer, Lye Tuck-Po, explains that, for them, trees can walk. They walk because they have roots which, as they grow, push themselves through the soil in just the same way that people, in their walking, lay down paths through the tropical rainforest. We find the same idea over and over again – in the ethnography of Aboriginal Australia as well, in the whole idea of song-lines. The same idea kept popping up – so often, indeed, that you begin to wonder why anthropologists haven't cottoned onto it before. Why haven't they noticed that this idiom of the line as a way of life appears in just about every society under the sun? 'Why not go with this idea,' I thought, 'and see where it takes us.' Thinking about lines was thus a perfectly natural development from the way I was thinking about life as a movement.

This does raise a problem, however. The problem is: what happens if you can't actually see – or in any other way perceive – this line of movement?

People have asked me this in terms of, say, the difference between moving on land and over water. What happens, for example, as Sámi people make their way in a landscape of forests and lakes? They might at one moment be walking along a trail through the forest, and at the next have to take a rowing boat across a lake, before picking up the trail again from the other side. You can see the trail in the woods but not in the lake, because the wake of the boat is immediately dissolved. Yes, the trail is still there, I thought, but it exists in memory rather than being physically present in the world. This is still a really tricky problem, however. We can speak of lines of life, and of how as we move about we leave a trail, but just how that trail is instantiated in the world can vary depending on the kinds of surfaces and materials one has to deal with. Laying down the line should perhaps not be interpreted too strictly, because otherwise what do you do if you can't see any line and nothing appears to have been laid down? It just pushes the question to 'What has been laid down then, and where?' The line becomes a question with no ready-made answer. That's what makes it so generative.

Philip Tonner

Now to my next question. You have referred to wayfarers as having their being in movement, or more exactly, that wayfarers are continually on the move, they *are* their movement. Also, you have referred to wayfinding as a feeling through a world, knowing one's way thanks to narratives of journeys previously made. On this view mapping emerges as a kind of re-enactment. Can you explore the role of stories and songs in this process, and how does this relate to your account of sensory education? Finally, are wayfarers necessarily travellers?

Tim Ingold

Stories and songs, I think, are forms of wayfaring. Telling a story is similar to walking along a path. They often go on together, as when the story is told as you walk along the path. Australian Aboriginal people are famous for this. They tell stories of the exploits of their ancestors, even as they walk through the very landscape that the ancestors created in their activities. Here the singing, the storytelling, the walking, all proceed at once.

But this does suggest something about how we should understand stories. This might be clear to anthropologists, but it's not often so clear to people in the field of literary studies, for example, who tend to think that a story, in order to qualify as narrative, has to have a beginning, a middle and an end. It needs to have some sort of plot. The thing about stories as forms of wayfaring, however, is that they don't have a beginning, and they don't have an end. There are places you move through. But, just as in life, stories don't start and they don't stop, they just carry on, beginning from nowhere in particular, carrying on for a while, and then disappearing again. Nobody actually knows how they begin and how they end. That's how it should be. The way I think about the story is as a kind of loop. It's as if you take a thread, loop it back on itself, pick up a stitch and pull through. You might say that at one end, what's going on is life, and at the other end, it's story. But you can't say where the story ends and life begins, because life is simply carrying the story on. So, when it comes to the story you have a looping back into the past and a pulling through into the present. If the story is a loop, then it's all of the same yarn, of the same thread as life but, like life, 'it doesn't have a starting point or an end point.

Importantly, then, the role of stories is not to pass on information from one generation to the next. It is often supposed, even by anthropologists, that stories are a means of education and that cultural norms, cultural standards, core values, are encoded in them. The stories are told; the children hear the stories, somehow manage to decode them and pick up the information that's been pre-packaged inside. I think this is completely wrong. Stories don't come with meanings already coded into them; rather, the meaning of the story, or of an incident related in it, is something that listeners discover for themselves, often long after the telling, when they find themselves in a situation which calls it to mind. Then, and only then, as its meaning becomes clear from the situation at hand, does the story offer guidance on how to proceed.

We would do better, then, to compare the passing on of stories to handovers in a relay race, in which one story carries on from another, and another from that, and so on along an unbroken line, so that the story of stories continually unfolds. This is connected to the question of sensory education, because it leads us to think of education as a way of carrying on along this path of exploring the world, rather than as the acquisition of cultural models for interpreting it. Sensory education is primarily about tuning the senses, or teaching people to pay attention to this, that, or the other thing, which may turn out to be important for keeping the story going.

Are wayfarers necessarily travellers? That's a really interesting question. It's a question of whether you could fare in your imagination, without actually having to go anywhere. Maybe. The philosopher Immanuel Kant would not have approved of my way of thinking, but he was nevertheless very proud of the fact that he could talk about almost everywhere in the known world without once having to leave his native Königsberg. So maybe he was a wayfarer who didn't travel. One can think of other examples like that. But for my part, I've mostly thought of wayfaring and travelling as one and the same. You might be right, however. It might be possible to be a wayfarer but not to travel at all. You could read books instead, and travel in your mind.

Philip Tonner

Thank you, Tim. Next question then. Most recently, you have begun to write under the banner of 'correspondences'. Here, you attempt to correspond with things themselves in the very processes of thought. Can you explain what you mean by this?

Tim Ingold

For me, correspondence means going along together with other things or beings, and answering or responding to them as you go. I could explain it, first, by contrasting it with the more familiar and commonly used concept of interaction. Interaction is a back-and-forth oscillation, like ping-pong. I say something to you. You say something back to me. I say something back to you. We go back and forth. We usually suppose, in archetypical situations of interaction, that we would be standing or seated face to face. It's a tense and possibly threatening situation, since each party in an interaction can see behind the other's back.

But with correspondence, it's as though we were walking along side by side. Imagine two people walking down the street, having a conversation. They are not looking directly at one another, although each might tilt their head a little towards their companion. As they walk and talk along together, they share the same view ahead, while neither can see what lies behind their backs. This going along together and responding to one another as you go is correspondence. But suppose that these two friends, walking down the street, suddenly start arguing. They stop in their tracks, and each turns through a right angle to face the other. They can no longer move forward because, if they did, they would bump into each other. In interaction, the participants are stationary. Only the words, or the goods, go back and forth between them. The people themselves are stuck.

Whereas interaction, then, is the back-and-forth of words, or of goods, between two people, each of whom occupies a position, in correspondence the two people are lines which, as they unfold, continually answer to one another. Another example which I've sometimes used is the fugue in musical counterpoint, in which the different melodic lines carry along together and respond to one another. I have found this helpful for thinking about how a world of things and people can unfold over time.

Another word that many use, and which has become very fashionable, is 'intra-action'. It comes from the work of the feminist science scholar Karen Barad. Although she is getting at much the same thing as I am, I don't like the term so much. This is because intra-action turns the 'inter' into an 'intra'. Instead of going back and forth, it's going out and in, out and in. This is hard to enact gesturally but, in effect, it's the inverse of interaction. It involves a shift of 180 degrees. But with correspondence, the shift is of only 90 degrees. It is from the transverse to the longitudinal, from crossing between the banks of the river to joining with the waters in their flow. 'Intra-action' doesn't capture this feeling of going along, nor does it convey the sense of mutual responsiveness which, for me, is critical.

(C) IMAGINATION AND REALITY

Robert Gibb

As we discussed in the interview on 'Environment, Perception and Skill' (Conversation 3), your work has often sought to dissolve the distinctions or oppositions that are such a striking feature of western modernity. In your most recent book, you tackle the opposition between 'imagination' and 'reality', and set out to heal what you see as the 'rupture' between them in modern thought. Please can you tell us more about how you came to reflect more on imagination and what you mean by 'imagining for real'?

Tim Ingold

I came to reflect on this because readers, especially of *The Perception of the Environment*, would often say to me: 'I like your argument about perception. And I like that you've found a way to talk about perception that doesn't reproduce an absolute divide between humanity and non-humanity. But where in your theory do you put imagination?' That would be the question. And I didn't know how to answer. All I could do is promise to work on it! The question kept forcing itself on my attention: how can I deal with imagination in such a way that it doesn't reproduce the very distinction between humans and the non-human world that I had worked so hard to overcome? The easy, but facile response would be to say that human beings are uniquely endowed with a capacity to imagine, to reflect upon their existence in the world, which is evident from the wealth of symbolism, art and so on that no other creature has. To explain imagination in those terms, however, would take me right back to square one, to where I had started from.

The problem was to find a more satisfactory way of answering this question of imagination, which wouldn't end up resorting to an essentialist belief in human uniqueness, of the kind we've inherited from the Enlightenment. I'm not sure I have found the answer yet. I keep returning to the thought that perhaps there *is* something peculiar about the way humans get along in the world. That's probably true. But with *Imagining for Real*, I was looking for a vocabulary that would take us beyond the opposition between the real and the imaginary. Neither word is quite adequate – neither the word 'reality', nor the word 'imagination' – particularly when we define them in terms of their opposition. I'm really looking for something that is neither of these, something that no longer requires us to oppose these two domains to one another. I decided, as a kind of workaround, to call it 'imagining for real'. This doesn't mean conjuring something up in my head, and pretending that it physically exists 'out there'. What I'm getting at is neither imagined nor real, in the sense implied by their opposition; it's something else altogether, if only I could put my finger on what it is! I admit, in the book, that 'imagination' is not the best word to use. This is because it includes the word 'image', and for most of us, an image is some kind of representation of something else. And that is precisely what I do *not* intend with 'imagining for real'. Nevertheless, we have no alternative but to work with the vocabulary that our language has given us, and the word 'imagination' is no exception.

That, anyway, is why I found myself having to reflect more and more on this question. I just couldn't avoid it.

Robert Gibb

The first part of the book is called 'Creating the World'. What do you understand by 'creation', and how is this different from the very commonly used notion of 'creativity'?

Tim Ingold

For me, creation is the process of the world's becoming world, its self-generation or autopoiesis. It is the cosmological idea of a world that is continually becoming; everything in that world is becoming as well; it's part of the whole process. And this becoming is generative. It is the continual coming-into-being of the *absolutely new*, by which I mean a newness that cannot be factored out as a combination of elements that went before. That's how I understand creation. My argument is that the creation of the world is devalued, almost trivialised, by its reduction to creativity – that is, to the output of some kind of cognitive faculty located in the architecture of the brain. This idea is very prominent in contemporary cognitive psychology, in which the literature on creativity is massive. On closer examination, it turns out that what cognitive psychologists mean by creativity is a mental faculty to recombine elements of existing knowledge into novel permutations and combinations. That's all there is to it. It's not about bringing forth a world, it's not about the creation of the absolutely new, it's not about becoming; it's simply a faculty of recombination. That's why biologists, for example, are so hooked on the idea of genetic recombination, as if that's all there was to the evolution of life. For psychologists it is just the same, except the recombination is not of genes but of ideas.

I wanted to resurrect the other side of creation, the side that is *not* captured by the combination and recombination of elements. I was particularly struck by a remark of the Franciscan friar and philosopher William of Ockham, writing in the fourteenth century. It is as ridiculous, said Ockham, to attribute creation to creativity as it is to attribute laughter to a faculty of risibility. Would you say, when somebody laughs, that this just proves they are endowed with a faculty of risibility, of which laughter is but an expression? As Ockham pointed out, laughter exists only in the laughing. Likewise, if there's anything we could call creativity, it lies in the creation itself. It is not a faculty that gives rise to things, but is inherent in the very process of *giving rise* itself. Only by restoring this sense of creation can we open up a future for coming generations that is truly generative. If anything has put the lid on future generations, and blighted their prospects, it is this notion of creativity. It puts all the emphasis on final products, on commodities, on novelties, and banishes the sense of renewal, of life that can bring further life. To have any coherent vision of sustainability, I believe, we need to recover this sense of life-begetting-life.

Robert Gibb

I was just thinking there about the meaning of 'the new' and the way in which, certainly in academia, much talk about 'creativity' amounts to reinventing the wheel, ignoring the work of predecessors.

Tim Ingold

Yes, absolutely. There's a key distinction, which I think goes back to the philosophy of Henri Bergson, between 'newness' and 'novelty'. Novelty is about ends, but newness is about beginnings. The point is that we need to re-establish the idea of life as a process of continuous birth, continuous generation. It is not simply a sequence of novelty projects. A baby, for example, is not a novelty to play with like a toy, but a new life, born into the world.

Robert Gibb

Imagining for Real ends with a chapter entitled 'One World Anthropology'. What do you mean by 'one world anthropology', and what do you think are some of the challenges facing its further development?

Tim Ingold

I'm rather against the fashion, in anthropology and other humanities and social sciences, to multiply worlds all the time, to put everything in the plural, to say that there are all these different cultural worlds: I'm in my world, you're in yours and everyone else is in theirs. It's the same when scholars bang on, in their inimitable jargon, about multiple epistemologies. This came out in discussion during a recent education conference I attended. Someone was saying 'We have all these students arriving, we need to recognise that everyone has their own epistemology.' Wait a moment! What sense does it make to say that every single person, or every single cultural group, or every single community, is enclosed in their own epistemological bubble? That would be politically unconscionable, because it would take away the responsibility to care for others and for how they're living. It seems to me that politically, morally, ethically, we *have* to start from the premise that we're all fellow inhabitants of this planet – 'we all' meaning not just humans, of course, but everyone and everything else – and that somehow or other we have to carry on a life together. That's what we *have* to do; it's a life task. We're born into this world someplace, sometime, not through any choice of our own, and somehow or other we have to keep everything going. This is a process for which we bear a collective responsibility. Of course, we're more responsible for people who are close to us, but everybody's in the same boat in that respect.

So, by 'one world', I mean that we all exist on this single planet. We should never forget that. The challenge, then, is to explain precisely what we mean by the one-ness of this world. It clearly is not the one world of, say, British Airways, or telecommunications, or corporate industry, or the graticulate logo of the World Bank. We're not talking about a single unity, and I don't think it helps to speak, for example, of a single, hyperconnected global village. What I want to say instead is that this is a one-world of manifold and ever-emerging difference. The key point is that difference does not mean division. Difference is the glue that holds relationships together. It is *because* we are different that we can relate to one another, that we can have conversations with one another, that we can move on. If we were all the same, then what would we have to talk about? We'd be stuck. We can move on because we have different experiences of life, and can exchange or share these in conversation. In this one world of ever-emerging difference, we are not divided up into people of this kind and of that. Rather, we are joined in relations of correspondence. It is through these relations that difference continually emerges. Thus, the one-ness of the world is in truth a multiplicity.

I'm not the only anthropologist saying this. Arturo Escobar, for example, has been talking a lot about the idea of the 'pluriverse'. It's an idea that has come down to us from the philosophy of William James, who coined the term in the first decade of the twentieth century. James was not saying that there are lots and lots of universes; he was saying there is a singular pluriverse, meaning that this one world we're all in is continually extending, ravelling and unravelling in limitless ways. There's no end to it, yet it is still one – one tapestry or weave, or whatever you prefer to call it. Pluriverse is not a bad word for it; I'm quite happy to use it in this sense. What I'm *not* happy with is a particular interpretation that is sometimes put on the pluriverse, epitomised by the call of the Zapatista movement in Mexico, for 'a world where many worlds fit'. Taken literally, this suggests that there are lots of little worlds squashed into this one big one. Perhaps we are not meant to take the formula quite so literally. But to me, at least, it doesn't sound quite right. The whole point about the one world is that it is *not* a container, into which things must be made to fit. On the contrary, the fabric of the pluriverse is an open weave.

Philip Tonner

I have two questions based on themes you cover in *Imagining for Real*. First, given your discussion of creation and creativity, how might you approach matters of religious belief (or, indeed, religious believers) in something like the God of classical theism? Second, you discuss several historical figures (Aquinas and Ockham, to name just two), as well as history itself. How might historians influenced by your work deploy it in their own investigations?

Tim Ingold

Those are big questions! Having come from a thoroughly atheistic or at least agnostic family background, and being a person of no fixed faith, I've sometimes surprised myself by how often, particularly recently, I've found that I am moving into waters that sound very theological, and finding in the writings of some theologians, or some philosophers of religion, echoes of what I think myself. This has been a surprise. The echoes are usually with those, like Aquinas, who say that what God created was existence itself, and that when we find ourselves in the midst of a world that is undergoing creation all around us, that, in itself, is an experience of God. I find myself entirely in sympathy with this view. If a theologian were to explain to me: 'Well, what we mean by God is really a kind of ever-emerging cosmos, which is irreducible, in which we find ourselves; and when we marvel at every moment at what it brings forth, that indeed is an experience of God,' I'd say: 'I get that. I would be perfectly happy to translate what you're calling God into my terms', and there wouldn't really be any disagreement. The only place where disagreement would creep in would be if the theologian were to claim it all to be a matter of belief. For me, belief is precisely where the problem lies. Because with belief, it is no longer a matter of experience. It is rather something you hold in your head, some sort of knowledge, or even some sort of hypothesis you might have about the world, to be put to the test. And that is absolutely *not* what it's about!

I think the word 'faith' comes closer to it. It's not about adopting some sort of propositional attitude towards the world; it's about being prepared to participate in worldly existence. This entails a certain existential risk; you have to put your life on the line, so to speak; you have in a sense to surrender to existence. If that's what God is, well then, you're surrendering to God. But that, then, is a question of faith, not one of belief. To render faith as belief is almost to put that faith in question, to say: 'Well, you *believe* it, but . . .' Whereas faith, as I understand it, is about being ready to take that existential risk of surrendering your own existence to existence writ large, that is, to God. In this regard, I think what I'm saying about creation fits in very well with certain forms of practical theology, but not so well with more doctrinal forms of Christianity or other religions. I wouldn't want to have any dealings with 'the Church', for example, but I don't mind having discussions about the existence and experience of God! That, I think, is my position. But it continually catches me by surprise how theologians turn out to have been writing about just the sorts of issues I've found myself having to address.

As for historians, I suppose it comes down to the question of what we take history to be. History for historians is somewhat limited in rather the same way anthropology is for anthropologists and philosophy for philosophers: in all these disciplines, scholars are in some sense bound by conventions which limit the scope of imagination. I have certainly found this with anthropology, and I think philosophers have a very similar problem. We need to find a different way of doing history, which wouldn't be so far from what I've been trying to do in thinking of a different way of doing anthropology, or what some philosophers are trying to do in finding a different way of doing philosophy. I'm not quite sure what it is, and it doesn't mean that traditional history or traditional anthropology or traditional philosophy is wrong or useless. We still need it in a way, but it would be good if we weren't *limited* to it. I am inclined to go back to Marx's famous statement in the Eighteenth Brumaire, of 1852, that 'men make their own history but not under circumstances of their own choosing, but under circumstances given from the past'.[2] Most of history and anthropology and sociology, I think, is really just a footnote to this. But I do wonder what would happen if, instead of 'men' or 'people', we put 'living beings'? What if we said, 'living beings make their own history, not under circumstances of their own choosing, but under circumstances given from the past'? And what if that history were actually the very same thing as what we've been calling evolution? What if so-called history were just a special case of an evolutionary process, not of a Darwinian kind, but of continual world-creation? That would be truly exciting. If only we could somehow get historians out of their history rut and get them to see

2 Marx (1963).

things on a broader canvas. But it's a tricky question. It is not for me to tell historians what to do!

Robert Gibb

You have described *Imagining for Real* as the final volume of a trilogy, along with *The Perception of the Environment* (2000) and *Being Alive* (2011). In the 'General Introduction' to the book, you reiterate a point you've also emphasised in your interviews with us: 'I have relished the freedom to go where the wind blows, without having to be registered under any disciplinary flag, living the life of a buccaneer on the high seas of scholarship.' Now, with the arguably greater freedom that retirement brings (at least with respect to the 'audit culture' of the contemporary university), where do you think the wind is likely to blow you next?

Tim Ingold

I took a quick look at the REF[3] results yesterday, and I thought to myself: 'Thank goodness I'm free of all that!' In fact, I'd completely forgotten about it, and then I remembered: 'Oh yes, the REF.' At the end of it, after the time and energy wasted on this totally unproductive effort, which yields nothing in terms of improved knowledge or understanding, we at the University of Aberdeen came out more or less exactly where we were last time. What on earth was the point of it all? I'm sure the great majority of our colleagues across Higher Education in the UK have the same feeling. I'm really glad to be out of it – able to write what I want to write, think what I want to think, publish what I want to publish. I have finished this trilogy, and I don't see myself doing another book of essays on such a scale, so that's it wrapped up.

---

3   REF stands for 'Research Excellence Framework', a UK-wide regime of research assessment, carried out every few years, which covers all subject areas in every institution of higher education in the country. The latest set of results was published in 2022.

There's a short-term and a long-term answer to your question. The short-term answer is that this year I'm going to write a very short book, for Polity Press, called *The Rise and Fall of Generation Now*. This will basically be about the way we think of the passage of generations. I've become convinced that one of our big problems in addressing issues of sustainability, climate change, artificial intelligence, the future of the world and all of that, is that we're still thinking of generations as layers which supersede one another. I want to ask: what happens if instead we think of generations as winding around one another, like the strands of a rope, so that the old and the young could collaborate in making a common future for all? By 'Generation Now', I mean the generation of adults which has forced its way in between children and old people, who hold all the cards and claim to be the ones making history. To the generation of children, Generation Now insists that they need to be socialised into a future prepared for them, to old people, it says 'You've had your time, it's time for you to jump off the bus.' There are reasons why this view of life has become established. It's very heavily enshrined in our institutions, in our educational systems and so forth. In my view, it gets in the way of thinking creatively about the future. Why do we always assume that the problem of the future is one that calls for techno-scientific solutions? Why don't we think of it in terms of kinship and descent? These are the sorts of issues I'll address. Some of this will be a spin-off from *Imagining for Real*, particularly the chapter called 'The World in a Basket'.

Having done all that, what I'm really meaning to do is to cast all this theoretical stuff aside, go back to Lapland and pick up on fieldwork that I was doing in 1979–80 and never properly wrote up. I have all the fieldnotes in boxes on my floor. I'll need to go back to the archives, talk to a few people, do a bit more fieldwork and write a proper ethnography of the place. I owe it to the people to do that. So that's a long-term retirement project. Having said all these things about ethnography – that we shouldn't be reducing anthropology to ethnography – I shall nevertheless reinvent myself as an ethnographer again! After all, why not?

Further reading

Ingold's writing on human–animal relations ranges from one of his earliest publications, 'On Reindeer and Men' (1974), through his *Hunters, Pastoralists and Ranchers: Reindeer Economies and Their Transformations* (1980) and the edited volume *What is an Animal?* (1988), to his influential article 'From Trust to Domination: An Alternative History of Human–animal Relations' (1994). He revisited the theme in his Westermarck Memorial Lecture, 'Anthropology Beyond Humanity' (2013). His early explorations of the relations between social and ecological systems are contained in his first essay collection *The Appropriation of Nature: Essays on Human Ecology and Social Relations* (Ingold 1986b).

What is an Animal? (Ingold 1988a) was one of four volumes arising from the theme 'Cultural Attitudes to Animals, Including Birds, Fish and Insects' in the 1986 World Archaeological Congress. The others were: *The Walking Larder*, edited by Juliet Clutton-Brock (1989), on the topic of domestication; *Signifying Animals*, edited by Roy Willis (1990), on the topic of animal symbolism, and *Animals into Art*, edited by Howard Morphy (1989), on the topic of representation. Ingold mentions the classic works on humans and animals by philosopher Mary Midgley (1978, 1983), but readers may wish to start with *The Essential Mary Midgley* (2005), edited by David Midgley. Other landmark studies to which Ingold refers include Lewis Henry Morgan's *The American Beaver and his Works* (1968) and A. Irving Hallowell's 'Ojibwa ontology, behavior and world view' (1960). He also refers to the work of Jakob von Uexküll, whose essay *A foray into the worlds of animals and humans*, dating from 1934, is republished, along with his 1940 essay *A theory of meaning*, in Uexküll (2010). Von Uexküll's ideas have been recently revisited in the work of Eduardo Kohn, *How Forests Think: Toward an Anthropology Beyond the Human* (2013).

On the questions of language, intentionality and consciousness in humans and animals, Ingold refers to the works of linguist Noam Chomsky, in *Rules and Representations* (1980), philosopher John

Searle, including 'The Intentionality of Intention and Action' (1979) and *Minds, Brains and Science* (1984), sociologist Anthony Giddens, in *Central Problems in Social Theory* (1979), and anthropologist Michael Jackson, in *Paths Toward a Clearing: Radical Empiricism and Ethnographic Inquiry* (1989). A comprehensive statement of Ingold's own position, at this stage of his career, can be found in his article 'Social Relations, Human Ecology and the Evolution of Culture: An Exploration of Concepts and Definitions' (Ingold 1996c).

Ingold's two books on lines are: *Lines: A Brief History* (2007a) and *The Life of Lines* (2015). André Leroi-Gourhan's *Gesture and Speech*, dating from 1964–5, appeared in English translation in 1993. Ingold published a lengthy review of the work, '"Tools for the Hand, Language for the Face": An Appreciation of Leroi-Gourhan's *Gesture and Speech*', in 1999. In his discussion of lifelines, Ingold refers to studies by James Weiner, *The Empty Place: Poetry, Space and Being among the Foi of Papua New Guinea* (1991), Claudio Aporta, 'Routes, trails and tracks: trail breaking among the Inuit of Igloolik' (2004), Tuck-Po Lye, *Knowledge, Forest and Hunter-Gatherer Movement: The Batek of Pahang, Malaysia* (1997) and Bruce Chatwin, *The Songlines* (1987).

Ingold first set out his position on correspondence in his essay 'On human correspondence' (Ingold 2017c). His essay collection *Imagining for Real: Essays on Creation, Attention and Correspondence*, was published in 2022 (Ingold 2022a). On the concept of intra-action, see Karen Barad's *Meeting the Universe Halfway: Quantum Physics and the Entanglement of Matter and Meaning* (Barad 2007). William James proposed his idea of the pluriverse in a lecture delivered in 1908, and published as *A Pluralistic Universe* (James [1909] 2012). Anthropologist Arturo Escobar has recently taken up the same idea in his book, *Designs for the Pluriverse: Radical Interdependence, Autonomy and the Making of Worlds* (2018). Ingold's latest book, *The Rise and Fall of Generation Now*, was published in 2024.

CONVERSATION 5:

Looking back and forward

> **Summary:** In this conversation, Ingold looks back over his career to date and indicates the directions in which he intends to pursue future work. Specifically, Ingold discusses his attempts to integrate or synthesise different fields at different stages in his career; his approach to teaching; the key challenges facing anthropology today; what he has learned from colleagues and students; and what he plans to work on next. The interview took place on 13 November 2020.

Robert Gibb

In a 'Research Statement' you kindly shared with us, you point out that one recurrent feature of your career to date has been the attempt to 'integrate' or 'synthesise' anthropology with a range of different fields or disciplines: for example, evolutionary biology, ecological psychology, art, architecture and design, education. How would you explain this feature of your career?

Tim Ingold

I suppose it goes back to the reasons that led me into anthropology in the first place. My recollection of what I was thinking when I decided to give up natural sciences and move into anthropology could well be coloured by a degree of wishful thinking and retrospective embellishment, so I might be burnishing the account a little. I do nevertheless remember having been greatly troubled, even at that time, by the division between the arts, humanities and social sciences, on the one hand, and the natural sciences and engineering, on the other. I belonged to a college in Cambridge, Churchill College, which was heavily biased towards science and engineering, and in which the humanities were in the minority. It was the time of the Vietnam War and I was struck not just by science's evident collusion with the military–industrial complex, but also by its sheer hubris – its confidence that it knew better than anyone else, and that it could be relied upon to produce technical solutions to any problem, even problems largely of its own making. Scientists and engineers, it seemed, were simply not interested in the real experience of real human beings. They weren't listening.

I was seeking a discipline that would transcend this division between the natural sciences and the humanities. I took a look at the possibilities, and two options stood out: one was the history and philosophy of science and the other was anthropology. I liked the look of anthropology, because it not only seemed to build a bridge between the sciences and the humanities; it also sought to do so in a way that remained close to real lives.[1] In this, I imagined, lay anthropology's very *raison d'être*. So that's why I decided to take it up. Having completed the first year of natural sciences at Cambridge, I was allowed to do my first year all over again, in archaeology and anthropology. Students in those days would start with courses in social anthropology, physical anthropology and archaeology. Then, from the second year on, you would decide in which of these three fields you would proceed. Naturally, I chose social anthropology. But I was fascinated by archaeology and physical anthropology as well. And the fact that these latter fields were there in my formation from the outset is one reason why I have continued to look for ways of pulling them together.

1   See Conversation 1 for more on the choice of social anthropology as a subject of study.

But the other thing is that anthropology, as I see it, is not a discipline that can be pinned down within any orthodox academic division of labour. We often think of each academic discipline as occupying a particular segment in an imaginary Venn diagram, in which it has its own slice of the cake and deals with its own particular range of phenomena. But anthropology, I felt, isn't like that. Rather than taking a slice of the cake as its own, it offers a somewhat eccentric, unorthodox angle on the entire cake. It seems to me, therefore, that anthropology is constitutionally *in-between* all the other disciplines. One of the reasons I've stayed with anthropology, even though I have often felt that it has gone one way and I've gone another, is because it allows this intellectual freedom to roam, wholly unconstrained by disciplinary boundaries. When I talk with colleagues from other disciplines – historians, psychologists, biologists, whatever – they often regard my position with some envy; they say: 'I wish we could do that! I wish we could allow ourselves to wander off in directions we'd never anticipated. We're not allowed to do that in our discipline. We have to run on our particular tramlines.' The great thing about anthropology, I've always thought, is that you can live the life of an intellectual buccaneer on the high seas: basically, follow your nose and go anywhere you want. You're like a nomad scholar: you can pitch your tent anywhere, next to whatever you're interested in. You don't have a castle to occupy and defend. I've always valued that.

These are the reasons, I suppose. 'Integration' might not really be the right word; 'synthesis', I think, is better. Integration sounds very rigid. Synthesis carries the sense of fields being able to get along while negotiating their differences, rather than being bolted together into a grandiose structure that fixes everything in its place. Getting along means dealing with problems of language, of potential misunderstanding, allowing scholars, even when they differ, to converse with one another and reach some mutual understanding of what they are talking about.

Diego Maria Malara

You've obviously had a very long career; you've been a very prolific scholar and worked in different departments in a number of academic institutions. Throughout this long journey, who were and are your favourite anthropologists, and why?

Tim Ingold

I don't really know. I don't have any special favourites. In any case, they have passed in and out of favour with the passage of time. When I began, back when I was making up my mind whether to study anthropology, my father fixed up a conversation with the anthropologist Jean La Fontaine, who at the time was a colleague of his at Birkbeck College London. I spoke to Jean, and she was very helpful. She told me to read Fredrik Barth's book *Political Leadership Among Swat Pathans*. I read it and I was completely bowled over. I said to myself: 'Well, if that's what anthropology is, I'm doing it!' And indeed, for a long time Fredrik Barth was definitely my favourite anthropologist: he was a kind of guru for me, as he was for many others of my generation, especially in his native Norway. When I graduated and was deciding where to go for my doctoral research, I wanted to follow a Barthian approach. I firmly believed that in this approach, known as 'transactionalism', lay no less than the future of anthropology, and for that reason, I resolved to spend a period of time in Barth's department in Bergen, to study at his feet. I was proud to call myself a Barthian.

But by the time I returned from fieldwork, all that was over: transactionalism was dead, and neo-Marxism was now the new thing. I was very enthused by some neo-Marxist writings, the work of Maurice Godelier in particular. I took this work very seriously, as I thought it might offer a possible framework for integrating social and ecological theory. That was in the late 1970s and early 1980s, when the craze for neo-Marxism was at its height. But then it all fell apart, like a house of cards. From then on, my favourite authors –

the authors that were really guiding lights for me – were not anthropologists. They were writers like James Gibson in psychology and Maurice Merleau-Ponty in philosophy, and later on, in the 1990s, André Leroi-Gourhan, the French archaeologist and anthropologist of techniques. They were important figures for me.

The biggest influences, thus, came from outside anthropology – or at least, from outside *social* anthropology. I think this is revealing. When I was starting out, it was widely assumed that social anthropology had its own body of theory. Whether it came from a Barth or a Godelier or anyone else, this was social anthropological theory, and scholars from other disciplines would look to anthropology to find it. Archaeologists, for example, would often admit that while they were experts in the excavation and interpretation of prehistoric sites, they were at a bit of a loss when it comes to theory. So they would take their theory from social anthropology instead. But from the mid-1980s onwards, anthropology began to turn in on itself. It was all part of the debate on 'writing culture', initiated by James Clifford and George Marcus in their eponymous volume, published in 1986. Anthropology became very introverted. And the more introverted it became, the more it assumed an ethnographic and anti-theoretical posture. The theoretical self-confidence of previous generations simply evaporated. Instead, it was anthropologists who started going outside their discipline in search of theoretical inspiration. Anthropology became a net importer rather than a net exporter of theory. The really interesting, exciting theoretical developments always seemed to be coming from somewhere else. To an extent, I think this is still the case.

But then there was Marshall Sahlins! Everyone has some sort of relationship to Marshall Sahlins, or at least to his work. In fact, one of the first essays I read on commencing my studies in anthropology in 1967, had been authored by Sahlins, in a book co-edited with his colleague, Elman Service, entitled *Evolution and Culture*, and dating from 1960. I was hugely impressed by it, although my tutor at the time – the archaeologist and Indianist Raymond Allchin – warned me that I should never, ever read anything like that again! But later,

I would be teaching Sahlins's 1972 classic, *Stone Age Economics* to my own students. And in 1975, when he came to visit the University of Manchester, he was working on his *Culture and Practical Reason*, published the following year. Like many others, I was in awe of the man. 'I wish I could write like Sahlins,' I would say to myself. 'He's such a great anthropologist, and his writing is so witty and ingenious.' But then another voice in my head would say: 'Thank goodness I *don't* write like Marshall Sahlins!' There would always be these two voices competing with one another. One would say: 'It's really exciting and interesting and funny and captivating.' But then the other would counter: 'Wow, does this man *show off!* Is there really any careful thought and substance to all this, or is he just trying to be clever?' Thus, my reaction to Sahlins and his work was always very ambivalent.

However, you asked me which anthropologists were my favourites. It is actually easier to answer on the opposite side: which anthropologists are my *least* favourite? Here, the devil's chair is occupied by Clifford Geertz. I've always disliked Geertz's kind of anthropology. It's wordy, it's slippery, it's pretentious. So, he's the very opposite of my hero. I used to present Geertz's *Agricultural Involution*, from 1963, as an example of how *not* to do ecological anthropology.

Then, there are anthropologists who've been tremendously helpful: maybe not inspirational, but wonderfully supportive. People like James Woodburn, when I was getting into hunter-gatherer studies. Such a warm, generous, kind person! Not someone whose ideas are riveting, perhaps, but a really close, trustworthy colleague. After a while, however, the colleagues to whom you owe a debt of one kind or another simply become too numerous to name individually. If you were to ask me who my favourite anthropologists have been, over the last twenty or thirty years, my answer would have to be 'all my PhD students'. They are the people from whom I've learned the most, and most enjoyed working with. So it's a generational thing. You start off looking up to all these people who are a lot more senior than you – Barth, Godelier, Sahlins – but then, as you get older, the balance tips and you find that, well, the older generation is passing,[2] you're a bit tired of colleagues of your own age, but the really interesting and exciting people are in the next generation. But again, they're too numerous to list.

Robert Gibb

Could you tell us more about your approach to teaching more generally, and whether it's changed over the course of your career?

Tim Ingold

I'm sure it has changed, yes. But probably in its fundamentals, it hasn't. It's changed in the sense that one finds out through trial and error, and experience, how to do things right and how things can go wrong, what works and what doesn't. That's the same for everyone. I know what I'm *against*: I'm against the standard teaching and learning model, in which a teacher is simply there as a kind of operative to ensure the safe and easy transmission of knowledge from an authoritative source into student minds. In this standard model, you're expected to make things as easy for the student as possible, so that they will come out with the knowledge they're supposed to know, and not have to suffer too much. This is utterly absurd. Nowadays, with so much technology, it virtually turns the lecturer or the tutor into someone who presses the keys on the projection machine; they're simply there to mediate the transfer of knowledge from the source to the recipient.

---

2 Fredrik Barth, Marshall Sahlins and James Woodburn have all sadly passed away in the last few years. Barth passed in 2016 (see https://rai.onlinelibrary.wiley.com/doi/pdf/10.1111/1467-8322.12245); Sahlins in 2021 (see https://news.uchicago.edu/story/marshall-d-sahlins-titan-anthropology-1930-2021); and Woodburn in 2022 (see https://www.theasa.org/publications/obituaries/woodburn).

That is *not* what teaching is. To teach is to bring students along with you, as fellow travellers, on a journey of intellectual discovery which you undertake together, and which is transformative for everyone. That to me is what teaching is. I'm not there to transfer the knowledge into the students' heads; I'm rather there as some sort of expedition guide, who knows the ropes, is able to offer advice and is equipped to sort things out in case of emergency. As a teacher, I can say to a student: 'It's probably better to go this way rather than that, but we'll see.' I'm also quite traditional in that I think lectures are really important. Every lecture is an occasion that brings its audience together to witness a performance which, if it works, can be truly inspirational. The purpose of the lecture is not to transmit information, but to get students excited about the subject. Nothing works better than a good lecture to inspire students to think about a particular subject in new ways. It should not be packed with information, but should convey something of the sheer excitement of thinking of things for the first time.

That's my approach to teaching. But when I began in the early 1990s to read anthropological studies of learning, in the work of people like Jean Lave – anthropological studies of how people actually learn things in the ordinary course of life, in apprenticeship or at school – I realised that there's a huge disparity between the way teaching and learning are set up in a formal institutional context, such as a university, and what anthropologists are saying about how teaching and learning happens in real life. For example, Lave distinguishes between the *teaching curriculum* (this is in a school context), in which the teacher has the knowledge, which is on the syllabus, and has to make sure that it gets into the students' heads, and the *learning curriculum*, which is what is actually happening, the practical activities that really go on, not only between teacher and students, but also among the students themselves. This is about learning the ropes, including such things as how to manage in a classroom situation. That's what you learn in school, as well as the information.

I was teaching Jean Lave's work to students, and some of the more astute and critical of them were saying: 'Wait a moment: what Lave is saying is not what we're doing here. There's a contradiction between what anthropologists are saying about how learning actually happens in life, and what you're trying to do here, with your lectures and tutorials, where everything is set out, with you standing at the blackboard and writing things down, while we just have to sit and listen.' For me, the challenge was to restructure teaching in such a way that it would be compatible with what we know from anthropology about how learning actually works. That's what I tried to do. For example, in teaching the so-called *4As* course (Anthropology, Archaeology, Art and Architecture), I was experimenting with a way of teaching that would get away from the top-down teacher-to-student model, and replace it with a collaborative teaching-learning exercise in which everyone, in a sense, is working at things together.

That's my approach now. What then has teaching taught me about anthropology? What it has really taught me is this: that teaching is an essential part of *doing* anthropology. It's not just a chore we have to carry out in order to earn a living. Most anthropologists, in fact, spend much more time with students than they ever do in the field. But they project the practice of their discipline as if it were the other way around: as if they spent most of their time in the field, and only a bit of time in passing on the knowledge, derived from fieldwork, to students. The fact is that working with students is the main part of what we do, at least for those of us working in higher education. What I've learned is that if we are going to study with people 'out there', to study their experiments in living – which is, I think, what we're doing in anthropology – then we are under some sort of obligation, if we have been transformed by what we've learned, to give something back. How do we give things back? Not primarily through publication, but through teaching. If you were to wipe out the teaching and say: 'No, anthropology is basically the research we do, and the material we publish', we would simply have a half-empty, half-full discipline.

I feel really strongly about this. I think it is appalling that teaching is so often regarded as the delivery of second-hand goods. In some ways, it is the be-all-and-end-all of anthropology. That's why I've found myself arguing, in recent years, that we should replace ethnography with education as the principal objective of anthropology. Anthropology is fundamentally a way of education. We should place education front and centre, as the very purpose of anthropological inquiry.

I've also learned always to treat students as human beings who are just as intelligent as I am; they may not have read as much, and don't perhaps know as much about the discipline as I do, but that doesn't make them any less intelligent. You don't have to talk down to students; indeed, you really shouldn't! Never suppose that you have to make things simple for students so they'll understand. This merely confirms the idea that so many students have of themselves – because it has been drummed into them since school – that they are ignorant, and in need of knowledge from their elders to make up the deficit. This assumption is so deep-seated that it really needs to be tackled head-on. Real education begins not in ignorance but in not-knowing, and these are completely different.

Robert Gibb

Have you encountered any resistance to your approach to teaching and learning from the institutions you've worked in, or from colleagues or students?

Tim Ingold

No, I haven't really encountered much resistance. But I *have* come up against a kind of apathy or indifference. For example, when you want to put on a new course, you are required to make a formal proposal which goes through various committees. When I began with the 4As course, I felt sure that there would be objections. Yet, in fact, it went through without any problems. It was enough to have filled out the forms correctly and ticked all the boxes. For the bureaucrats, that was all that mattered. There was no concerted opposition.

No-one really cared what I did! 'It's a bit weird, what you're doing,' they would say, 'but it doesn't bother us. 'There's a kind of business-as-usual mentality, where things just carry on under their own steam. I figured out that the only way to bring about change is just to go ahead and do it; maybe then some ripples will spread out to others. That's really what I've done. You sometimes have to trust yourself and hope for the best that things will work out. They don't always. There's a certain amount of risk, I suppose. But so long as you're prepared to take the risk, the students love it – or at least the interesting students love it – because it makes a real difference.

Diego Maria Malara

To change the topic slightly: from the perspective that your achievements afford you, what advice would you give to your younger self? (I don't mean you're not still young!)

Tim Ingold

Like most people, I guess, when I look back on my younger self I do so with red-faced embarrassment. Goodness me, I had no inkling, no understanding of such things as endemic racism; I had no understanding of colonial history; I had no understanding of gender inequality. I had a very protected upbringing in an upper-middle-class academic home. I went to a public school. I did get involved in some worthy causes like Amnesty International. But when I look back on this younger self, I see the product of a particular kind of very sheltered upbringing. I think my parents, perhaps because of their experience of raising my older sisters during the war, went to some lengths to shelter me from aspects of social life and history that could be unsettling. Although, being academic, they were unconventional in their way, they were also extremely conventional in class terms, and in attitudes to race and gender – all these things that are currently topics of so much angst, shouting and politics. None of that was known to me. It took a while to get my head around it all and to understand why other people could get so upset about things which I had never really experienced myself. I mean, I had never even visited the north of England, except for family holidays in the Lake District. I spent most of my time in the south, and you know the difference between the south and the north! When my wife and I first went to live in Manchester, when I got my job there, it was like another country. People were very friendly, very kind, but they would have to explain to us: 'This is how we do things here.' It was almost like fieldwork, landing in a place that was so completely unfamiliar in terms of culture and history. And that was just Manchester!

So, when I look back, I see someone incredibly naïve and inexperienced. And because I had done my fieldwork in Lapland, I had not had to confront the more brutal aspects of colonialism or violence on the scale you find in other parts of the world. Of course there has been a history of colonialism in Lapland, of relations between Indigenous Sámi people and mainly Finnish settlers, but it is one that has unfolded over many centuries, involving symbiosis as well as conflict. The experience of First Nations peoples in the Canadian North, for example, has been entirely different.

If I was now talking to my younger self, I would be trying to explain to this young man about all these aspects of history and society about which I was so naïve, and I would try to say: 'Look, you've got to think again about some of these things.' That, I suppose, would have saved me quite a lot of time. It wouldn't have taken me decades to come to terms with them. So that's one piece of advice. Other things I think I learned anyway, about teaching and about research. Having been brought up in an academic family, much of that was already familiar.

Diego Maria Malara

Since we are quite interested in kinship and generational continuity and discontinuity in anthropology, can I ask whether you sent your own children to public school?

Tim Ingold

Good heavens, no! I would never have dreamed of doing that. Our children went to state comprehensive schools. Let me explain. As you will recall from our first conversation, my parents sent me to Leighton Park School, a Quaker school near Reading. It's now co-educational, there are girls and boys. But at that time, it was just for boys. It was not only a single-sex school but also a public school in the British sense; you had to pay fees. But because it was a Quaker school it was imbued with the liberal values of Quakerism, which are, on the whole, pretty tolerable (and tolerant) compared with other variants of Christianity. We would probably agree that the sorts of values inculcated there were good ones. It was a generous, open environment – not in any sense oppressive. There was nothing like the atmosphere of oppression associated with the classic model of the British public school, and which you can read about from those who have gone through it. But it was a public school nonetheless, and still a rather exclusive community of very privileged young people.

We were very lucky, first in Manchester, where we brought up our three sons, and then here in Aberdeen, where we brought up our daughter. The local comprehensive school in Manchester – Parrs Wood High School – was fantastic. One of the reasons why it was fantastic, I suppose, was that it was in the middle of the area of the city most popular with university people. So, it had lots of very academically minded kids, as indeed ours were. Our children were fortunate in that they fell in with the right crowd. This was pretty much a happy accident. Others were not so fortunate, as the circulation of drugs among youngsters had already become endemic. Here in Aberdeen our daughter went to Aberdeen Grammar School, which, despite its name, has been a comprehensive school since the 1970s. It is also a fabulous school. So we've been lucky. But I think these schools absolutely prove the point that comprehensive education is on another level in terms of what it can achieve. Public schools might be good at getting their kids into top universities, but in purely educational terms they're failing by comparison with what good comprehensive education can do.

I think there were two reasons why I was sent to a public school. One was that I would otherwise have likely ended up in the local grammar school – these were the days before comprehensive education – which actually doubled up as a public school, and was much more traditional, rigid and authoritarian than the school I attended. The other reason was that my dad was away a lot of the time, gallivanting around Africa on university business. It was a bit like being the son of a diplomat, you never knew exactly where your parents were.

Diego Maria Malara

Moving on again: what in your view are the biggest problems in British and global anthropology today both in terms of theory and at the institutional level?

Tim Ingold

Let's start at the institutional level. As a small, slightly off-beam subject, anthropology has always been vulnerable institutionally. It is very easy for people who don't know anything about anthropology to query why we need it or what useful knowledge it has to contribute. We all know that anthropology has not been very good at managing its public image. We have made a pretty poor job of explaining to everyone out there what the subject is really about and what it does, why it's important, what it contributes. Even those working inside universities, particularly in administration and management, often have little idea of what anthropology is, or of why we should need it. The subject doesn't have the kind of assured recognition enjoyed, say, by history, geography, biology and so on. So if a situation arises when it is necessary to make cuts, anthropology can be first in the firing line. 'If we cut anthropology,' they say, 'nobody is going to notice. After all, what difference does it make?'

This has always been the case, and in times of contraction, such as during the Thatcher cuts of the 1980s and during the cuts we've been suffering in recent times, anthropology always seems to be at the sharp end. A lot can depend on student numbers, because these are the first beans that university administrators tend to count. And again, we're vulnerable to rather intense fluctuations in student numbers. They go up and down, depending on all sorts of factors which are completely outside our control: things to do with levels of employment, where the opportunities are and so on. There's nothing much we can do about it. Student numbers will go up and they will go down, and every time they go down, the position of anthropology is placed in jeopardy yet again.

This goes back to the point that in order to strengthen the position of anthropology, we really need to put more work into the effort of showing to a general audience, to the public at large, why anthropology is so important, why we cannot do without it. We have to be able to explain this. So far, we have not been very successful. This is not because we are bad communicators; it is because the kinds of things we have to say often challenge popular preconceptions. Popular science, like all good advertising, works by playing to its audience's preconceptions, spiced up with a twist of novelty. There is some truly dreadful writing in popular anthropology that does the same – I am thinking of bestselling authors like Jared Diamond and Yuval Noah Harari – and it has made our task even more difficult. But the problem is compounded, I think, by the fact that we have been less than clear in our own minds about the purpose of anthropology in today's world, with its many interrelated crises, including the current pandemic,[3] a climate emergency, manifestly unsustainable levels of inequality and a collapsing global market economy. The world's in a mess. And where is anthropology? It is nowhere to be seen.

Of course, many anthropologists are working hard on these problems and making major contributions, but they are still in the corners rather than the centre ground of public discussion. By and large, the

---

3   This interview took place on 13 November 2020, when the pandemic was at its height.

public doesn't know what we're doing, or why. It is undeniable that we have a problem in putting ourselves across. In my own view – which I know many colleagues would dispute – the problem lies in the unfortunate contraction of anthropology into ethnography, which began in earnest in the era of the 'writing culture' debate. Although the debate is largely behind us now, it has never completely gone away.

For example, I have just been reviewing a bunch of applications to the British Academy, for postdoctoral research fellowships. It is an interesting task, in so far as it conveys a sense of what the brightest and best of the up-and-coming generation of scholars, having just completed their doctorates, are most keen to do, and where they see their future research heading. Yet it is a task that also fills me with despair because so few of the projects proposed in these applications have what I would consider a real anthropological flair. I can't help feeling that something about the spirit of the discipline has been lost. It's hard to put one's finger on what it is, and of course there's always a gap between the kinds of things we write in research proposals, and what we end up doing in practice. Perhaps the problem actually lies in the research proposal format. Nonetheless, what invariably comes across is that the researcher intends to collect lots of ethnographic data on the people to be studied, to analyse the results and then to convert them into publications for academic journals, and perhaps a monograph. There is no sense in this that every way of life is itself an experiment in how to live, and that we can learn from these experiments. This means listening to, and learning from, what people have to tell us. It doesn't mean using what they tell us as ethnographic evidence, for what it tells about them.

I believe anthropology as a discipline draws on experiments in living, carried on by people everywhere and at all times, to inquire into the conditions and possibilities of human life in the world, both presently and into the future. That's what I think anthropology does, or at least should do. That's why it is so important. But I don't find it in the disciplinary formation of the current generation of doctoral students. To recover this sense of anthropological inquiry, which goes way beyond the particularities of ethnographic research, I think we should devote rather more attention than we do to our anthropological ancestors. Students nowadays have scarcely heard of Max Gluckman, Edmund Leach or Meyer Fortes – and these just from Britain – who were great names in their time, with frequent appearance on the BBC, and articles in national newspapers. These were people who had big things to say – about the unifying effects of cross-cutting conflict, about the fundamental importance of human connection, about love and kinship as the essence of social relations. We need to have that same level of ambition, and that's what I miss at the moment. There must be more to anthropology than high-end journalism. I think this is the biggest problem in anthropology today. The worst that could happen would be if it were to contract into an academic version of identity politics. Yet this often looks like the way it's going – especially in the United States, but elsewhere as well.

Philip Tonner

Going back to something you said earlier: what have you learned from your supervisees, your PhD students? Can you give us any examples?

Tim Ingold

My goodness! I have learned everything from my supervisees – really. I wouldn't know where to start. I counted them up recently, I have so far supervised 55 doctoral theses to completion.[4] Perhaps, rather than singling out specific individuals, I could just make a general point about why I have learned so much from them. It's not just because of what they're thinking, but also because of what they're

---

4 The final number, as of January 2023, was 61. I am no longer supervising doctoral students.

reading. You get to know work in all sorts of areas that you would otherwise have never encountered. And so, where to start? Well, just to give one example, which happens to be at the top of my head because I was writing about it only yesterday. One of my supervisees has been working on post-earthquake reconstruction in Northern Italy. He was reading literature on how people in late Roman and medieval times were building in the region, in such a way as to incorporate seismic protection into their constructions. This literature, on traditional building knowledge, was in fact written by architects and engineers. I found it fascinating because of the way it changes our assumptions about the very earth on which we build. Instead of seeing the surface of the earth as a solid platform, it appears fluid and unstable, more like the ocean. I would never have come to think of this had I not been supervising this work, and yet it has gone on to influence my thinking, quite profoundly, on issues of solidity and fluidity.

Probably my most brilliant PhD supervisee was working on perspectivism in Viking Iceland, among Shetland fishermen and in Amazonia. Had it not been for his work, I would never have come to think of the parallels between Indigenous Amerindian and medieval European philosophy. But there are just so many examples like this; I don't know where to begin! It's just that when you work with a student, you're not just reading what they write; you're actually having to delve into material in great depth. The job is to figure out what the argument behind it is, to bring a certain clarity to it and find the right words to express it, helping the student to articulate it in the best possible way. To do that you really have to get into the work, as if you were thinking and breathing it yourself, and to understand it from the inside.

So that's what I've learned. Really, it's about learning how to edit text, because the most important work of a supervisor is actually editorial. As a supervisor, you are an editor of a student's work in the full sense of the term – not just telling them where to put commas and full stops, but showing actually how to take an idea that is still half-formed and find the words to fill it out. And that's how you learn. It's impossible for me to summarise. I don't really want to give examples because that would mean picking on particular individuals and leaving out others.

Robert Gibb

Let's now move on to the question of writing. Do you think the way you write, and the way you go about writing, has changed over the course of your career?

Tim Ingold

Yes, it has. Writing is a very mysterious business. I suppose if I look back at things I wrote a long time ago, I can say: 'Oh yes, that looks like me'; I can see myself in it. But I had no particular competence in writing to begin with. You get an idea of how you should write from reading the work of much more senior people, but at first you lack any secure sense of your own way of writing. It took a long time for me to reach the point where I could say: 'This is actually *me* writing; it's not me pretending to be somebody else, or me trying to write in the way I'm supposed to write, or me following the model of this or that scholar. No, this is me and the writing is as distinctive to me as is my handwriting, or my voice.' It took me at least twenty years to get there. Then when I found what I thought was my voice, I would say: 'Right, that's me. I'm now going to try and build on it.' I definitely remember, at the start of all this, being advised to write in an almost novelistic way. I said: 'Well, I can't do that. I'm not a writer. I'm not a novelist. I can't do that kind of thing. I'm just an anthropologist, and I can only write in a matter-of-fact kind of way, as I've done in my fieldnotes. This is how it is.'

So I didn't feel that writing was a thing I was particularly cut out to do, least of all any better than anybody else, and at that stage I don't think I felt it was especially important either. But now I would take the opposite view: that writing is more important than anything else. I've realised that it's a process of discovery in itself. It's a process of self-discovery, as well as a discovery of the ideas that come over me as I write. I find it enormously satisfying to write beautifully. And that's what I try to do now. But the more I try, the more difficult it becomes. To write well is incredibly hard.

But things have changed in a practical way too. I hung on to writing by hand for as long as I possibly could. My doctoral thesis, of course, was entirely written by hand. I then had to type it all up on a manual typewriter. Later on, during those first years in Manchester, for the first decade or so, if you were writing a paper, you would first write it by hand and then pass it on to the faculty typing pool. This was a large room, filled with rows of small tables, on each of which was placed a typewriter. Seated at each table was a typist, invariably female, diligently clattering away on the keys, under the imperious supervision of the formidable but matronly woman in charge of the whole outfit. You would present your handwritten manuscript to the matron, who would then assign it to one or other of her ladies. When she'd finished, you would get it back and would have to check it through, correcting any errors with white correcting fluid, known as Tippex.

Then word processors came in, but I did my best to avoid them. I pretended to be outraged by the whole idea that writing could be a matter of processing words. But the real reason was that I had never learned to type properly. Indeed, I am still a two-finger typist. But the trend was irresistible, and I eventually found myself working on a keyboard like everyone else. But I hate myself for doing so, and for having become so keyboard-dependent. To my mind, the computer is nothing more than a box of shortcuts, and I do not believe we should take shortcuts in writing. We do it only because we are pressed for time, and always in a hurry. But that's not how it should be, and I still feel much happier writing by hand. Over the past couple of decades, I have developed a way of moving back and forth between pencil-and-notebook and keyboard. So, instead of writing longhand with pen on file-paper as I used to do, I now write with a pencil in a notepad and then go from sketches in the notepad to a more worked-out version on the keyboard.

There have been these very prosaic, practical changes in writing, because I started when even electronic typewriters had yet to be invented – there were only manual typewriters. Now, with laptop computers, the internet and all the rest, there have been massive changes in the whole process of writing. The one thing that hasn't changed, however, is my concern with the way writing sounds when you read it. I have always imagined that what I'm writing is something that will eventually be read out loud, as in telling a story. The sound matters and, in this, it's important to bring the reader along with you. That concern, I think, has always been there. But yes, writing has otherwise changed a lot.

Diego Maria Malara

Looking back on your career today, do you have any regrets?

Tim Ingold

Yes, lots. I was just thinking about this, and the main one is that I wish I could go back and do my first fieldwork again, perhaps with the Skolt Sámi people in northeastern Finland, among whom I carried out the fieldwork for my doctorate. At the time, I did what I thought I was supposed to do: concentrating on relations of kinship and neighbourhood, economic life, local-level politics. And I produced what in those days was regarded simply as a study in social organisation. People didn't call it ethnography then; it was merely a study of the organisation of a community. But to accomplish this I didn't need to learn the Skolt Sámi language properly. I picked the language up a bit, but only haphazardly. I never sat down with people to listen to all their stories. I didn't attend carefully to things like place names, or aspects of the landscape. These are topics in which I became interested much later on: language, landscape, perception, storytelling. But looking back, I realise that none of these topics was on my radar when I was doing my first fieldwork. It never occurred to me to sit down and work intensively with particular people from whom I could have learned about these things. And I really regret this, not least because many of those who were then elders in the community have now passed away. Much of what they knew has been lost. If only I had had a bit more foresight, I could have done something about it. I think that's my biggest regret. I was trained to do a certain kind of anthropological study and I simply did it without knowing what I could have done otherwise.

Other regrets have more to do with the fact that, basically, you can't have your cake and eat it too. Because I spent so much time doing X, I couldn't do Y. I sometimes think it's a pity I got so distracted by theory, when I could have been doing more fieldwork. I am by no measure a field anthropologist. I have done rather little fieldwork – perhaps three years of my life in total – and I cannot speak as many colleagues do who have devoted the best part of their lives to it. I didn't really sit down to decide on the way I wanted to go; I just found myself drifting in one way rather than the other. Perhaps that was all to the good, as I achieved things I would otherwise not have done. But it meant that other things got left on the sidelines, most particularly the follow-up fieldwork I carried out, again in Lapland, but with people of Finnish settler heritage. That was in 1979–80. I never wrote it up properly because I got sidetracked onto other things. It's another regret I have, as I feel I've let down the people with whom I was working. That's why I have this ambition to return there in a year or two, once the pandemic situation has stabilised, so I can pick up from where I left off. At least, the possibility is still there for me to make amends.

Philip Tonner

What are the anthropological theories and problems you find most exciting today and which are the ones that you're not so fond of, and why?

Tim Ingold

Oh, that's difficult to say! I mentioned earlier how hard I find it to get really interested in most of the proposals I was reading for the British Academy, in connection with their competition for postdoctoral fellowships. The same thing happens whenever I pick up the latest issue of *Journal of the Royal Anthropological Institute* and flick through the contents. I wonder, 'Is there anything of interest here?' Occasionally there is, but usually not. But then I ask myself: 'Why am I not interested? What's the matter?' And I don't really know. Part of the difficulty is that it has become increasingly difficult to pin theories to disciplines. If you think about the most exciting theoretical discussions going on just now, some do indeed start in anthropology and then filter through to other areas of the humanities and social sciences; others start in other disciplines and filter into ours. Let me give you an example. Currently, there is a lot of excitement around the ontological turn, new materialism and posthumanism. Like the points of a triangle, all three are connected. The ontological turn started off in anthropology, but has now spread all over the place. New materialism started in critical theory, feminism and literary studies, but it's spread into anthropology. Posthumanism likewise started beyond anthropology, mainly as a movement in philosophy, but has crept into anthropology too. These theoretical currents run in different directions, but they all converge and end up getting bundled together.

When I think about my own work, I suppose that in some respects, I have contributed to this particular bundle. From the late 1990s, I have been rethinking the idea of animism, arguing that we can no longer dismiss it as primitive belief. We should treat it, rather, as a sophisticated ontology in its own right. Today, this enterprise has been overtaken by the ontological turn. At the same time, I've been arguing that in the study of material culture, we should stop talking about objects all the time and instead take seriously the materials of which they are made. This has since become the mantra of new materialism. And yes, I've been thinking for a long time about the duplicity of received notions of humanity, and about how we might think the human otherwise, as a way of becoming rather than being. This kind of rethinking now comes under the fashionable moniker of posthumanism. I've been involved with all these developments, and have perhaps advanced them here and there. You would think, then, that these would be theoretical developments I find exciting, and indeed they are.

But when I read the literature emerging from these developments, especially perhaps when it is *not* produced by anthropologists (because anthropological work tends at least to be grounded in *something*), I find much of it utterly tendentious. It has largely lost touch with any of the grounded realities it claims to be addressing. Instead, it has become entirely self-referential, waffling on in a lazily metaphorical language which sounds very deep, and very clever, until you stop to ask what any of it actually *means*. Everything is 'embodied', forgetting that any living body breathes out as well as taking in; everything is 'entangled', forgetting that a tangle is of lines that are knotted together but don't connect; everything is 'imbricated', forgetting that imbrication is the way tiles overlap on a roof.

Partly as a result of this, the verb 'to theorise' has almost become a term of abuse. Literally, to theorise is to think: it is a way of thinking *with* the world, *in* the world. But in much scholarly literature, you have the feeling that this is the last thing its authors are doing. Rather, they are hiding behind their computer screens. 'Be phenomenological!' say these authors. 'Be *with* the world; be *in* the world.' It is all about being and becoming in the world, they say, or about 'worlding' – as it is now fashionably known. But you only have to read what they write to discover that it is about as far removed from the worlding world as you could possibly imagine. These scholars don't even try to practise what they preach, and it's very irritating. So if you ask me what I'm *not* particularly fond of, it's precisely this – the endless recycling of metaphors that have already lost touch with the ground from which they were originally derived, leading to writing that is not just impenetrable, but incomprehensible. It is bad writing, plain and simple, and there's a lot of it about.

Where things get exciting is when there is a vivid sense of direct encounter with real people, real organisms, real things, a real world. It's still theorising, but it's theorising in and with the world, not just about it. It is a theorising – a thinking – that arises from the encounter itself, not exclusively from the head of the theorist. That's why a lot of the work that I find most stimulating at the moment is on the boundary between anthropology and art, or performance, or architecture. These all offer ways of theorising the world from the very crucible of our existence as active and sentient beings within it.

The thing about art, as I put it in the 'invitation' to my book *Correspondences*, from 2021, is that rather than taking literal truths metaphorically, it takes metaphorical truths literally. Your typical academic theorist starts with some data, facts on the ground, but immediately lifts them off into the realm of metaphor, where everything is embodied, entangled or imbricated with everything else. But the poet starts from a metaphor and then digs down in search of the truth inside it. In my book I refer to a famous poem by Seamus Heaney, 'Digging', in which he compares his digging the pen into the surface of the paper as he writes with his father's digging for peat. He is likening his pen to his father's spade. He looks at his father bent over the spade, and he looks at himself bent over the words. That's a powerful metaphor for what it means to write, and for the effort, thought and care that go into it.

We know there's a truth buried in the metaphor. That's why the poem speaks to us. How, then, do we find that truth? We should go into the fields and dig! What do we learn from digging? What does digging tell us? Or: what does the earth tell us through the spade? *That's* the way to theorise – to ask questions like these, of the very earth we inhabit. I mentioned the word 'imbrication', which means the overlapping of tiles on a roof. But would any of the theorists who write earnestly about how things are imbricated be even prepared to learn from the experience of tiling a roof? Do they even care what the word actually means? The theoretical literature is full of metaphors that have completely lost touch with the ground from which they were originally drawn, at which point they lose all meaning. So, the question is not so much one of which *theories* am I most fond of, as of what kind of *theorising* am I most fond of? It's a theorising that thinks directly through things, through activity, through performance, in the world.

Philip Tonner

You've already hinted at this in a couple of your answers, but what are your plans for the future?

Tim Ingold

My immediate plans are that I have got two books to complete. One is a third book of longer essays, which will be called *Imagining for Real: Essays on Creation, Attention and Correspondence*. When it is finished, it will form a trilogy alongside *Being Alive* and *The Perception of the Environment*. Then I have to put together an edited volume to be called *Knowing from the Inside*, based on the project we had by that name.[5] Once I've got those things out of the way, and a lot of other bits and pieces, then I want to draw a line under all this art and architecture stuff, and plan my return to Lapland, as I told you at the end of our previous conversation. It all depends, I suppose, on the pandemic and other contingencies, but that's the plan.

Further Reading

In his article 'In Praise of Amateurs' (2021c), Ingold reflects on anthropology as a practice of nomadic scholarship, while his essay 'From Science to Art and Back Again: The Pendulum of an Anthropologist' (2018c) gives a broader view of his career. The anthropologist Fredrik Barth, whose influence Ingold discusses

---

5 The project, *Knowing from the Inside: Anthropology, Art, Architecture and Design*, was funded by the European Research Council and ran from 2013 to 2018.

near the start of the interview, is the subject of an intellectual biography by Thomas Hylland Eriksen (2015). Ingold also talks about the influence of Marshall Sahlins, including the early essay 'Evolution: Specific and General' (1960) and the books *Stone Age Economics* (1972) and *Culture and Practical Reason* (1976).

In his remarks on teaching and learning, Ingold refers to the work of Jean Lave, whose key publications include *Cognition in Practice* (1988) and, with Etienne Wenger, *Situated Learning: Legitimate Peripheral Participation* (1991). The course on the 4As (Anthropology, Archaeology, Art and Architecture), which Ingold taught at the University of Aberdeen, is discussed in Ingold with Lucas (2007). Ingold drew on his experience of teaching the course for his 2013 book *Making: Anthropology, Archaeology, Art and Architecture* (Ingold 2013a).

Ingold refers, inter alia, to the work of two of his doctoral students: Cesar Giraldo Herrera, on Viking and Amazonian perspectivism, and Enrico Marcore on post-earthquake reconstruction in northern Italy. He has developed his ideas on solidity and fluidity in collaboration with another of his former doctoral students, Cristian Simonetti, in a special issue of the journal *Theory, Culture & Society*, Volume 39 (2), 2022, entitled *Solid Fluids*, for which he co-authored the introduction (Ingold and Simonetti 2022).

On Ingold's contributions to the ontological turn, new materialism and posthumanism, see especially his essays 'Rethinking the Animate, Re-animating Thought' (2006) and 'A Circumpolar Night's Dream' (reproduced as Chapter 6 of *The Perception of the Environment*, 2011b/2000); 'Materials Against Materiality' (2007b) and 'In the Gathering Shadows of Material Things' (reproduced as Chapter 17 of *Imagining For Real*, 2022a); and Part III, 'Humaning' of *The Life of Lines* (2015) and 'Posthuman Prehistory' (reproduced as Chapter 20 of *Imagining for Real*, 2022a).

In his discussion of metaphor, Ingold refers to Seamus Heaney's poem 'Digging', dating from 1966 (Heaney 1990). The poem, along with Ingold's idea of taking metaphorical truths literally, features in the 'Invitation' to his 2022 collection, *Correspondences* (Ingold 2021b). In another essay in the collection, 'In defence of handwriting', he describes his own practice of writing and how it has evolved. Since this interview was conducted, both *Imagining for Real: Essays on Creation, Attention and Correspondence* (Ingold 2022a) and *Knowing from the Inside: Cross-Disciplinary Experiments with Matters of Pedagogy* (Ingold 2022b) have been published.

AFTERWORD

Tim Ingold

Let me begin with a question raised in the introduction to this volume. Why, throughout a career of writing, have I remained so reluctant to refer to material I have gathered through my own fieldwork? The majority of social anthropologists, surely, have been inclined to veer to the other extreme, returning obsessively to the people and places they know best from lengthy spells of field research. It is a legitimate question, and one that I have often asked of myself. In your reading of the foregoing conversations, you will doubtless have picked up many clues to possible answers. I would be the first to admit that the reasons are several, and that they are neither entirely consistent with one another nor derived from a coherent position that I could defend. Moreover, their salience has varied over time, such that the answers I might give now are not those I might have offered fifty years ago. Let me begin at the beginning, however, at the moment when my own doctoral research, with the Skolt Sámi of northeastern Finland, was on the point of completion.

It had long been conventional in anthropology to divide the world into so-called 'ethnographic regions'. Each region had its own body of literature, and would often be credited with having introduced a particular thematic focus or conceptual orientation into the anthropological mainstream. 'Central Africa', for example, was dear to the heart of the Manchester School, though when I joined the Department there, my new-found colleagues included specialists in 'East Africa', 'South Asia' and 'Europe', and subsequently 'Melanesia' and 'Latin America'. But my own region, known as 'the circumpolar North', was virtually unrecognised in British anthropology. Returning from the field, I thus found myself ethnographically homeless. An indication of my predicament came at the point when the authorities at the University of Cambridge had to select examiners for my doctoral dissertation. My external examiner, Ian Cunnison, had worked in the Sudan, with people who herded camels. My internal examiner, Caroline Humphrey, had worked in Mongolia, with herders of horses. The committee presumably imagined that by crossing camels with horses, and their respective regimes of herding, it might be possible to come up with something resembling Sámi reindeer pastoralism!

The shame and isolation, for a young researcher, of having no ethnographic home would be hard to exaggerate. It cut deep. It was certainly one reason why, in those early years, I felt almost embarrassed to talk about my material – a feeling of inadequacy only compounded by the cringeworthy title of my first book, based on my dissertation, *The Skolt Lapps Today* (1976). It came about because Cambridge University Press had decided to launch a new book series, all with the title *The* [name of people] *Today*. Thrilled to be offered a contract when the ink was not even dry on my thesis, I fell for it. I would have done better to wait. The series soon folded, whilst my book was forever tainted by my having called the people 'Lapps', just at the time when the worldwide campaign to replace exogenous ethnonyms with Indigenous designations was gathering steam. Sámi intellectuals, with good reason, were asking why anthropologists from abroad would invariably arrive in their countries to study people of their own kind rather than the majority of settler heritage. Could it be because the Sámi were assumed to be more exotically 'primitive'?

As it dawned on me that the motivations underlying my choice to study the Skolts were scarcely more honourable, I resolved to make amends by carrying out my next fieldwork in a Finnish community. This I did, in 1979–80, with a year's fieldwork in Salla, in eastern

Lapland, among people who combined reindeer herding with farming and forestry work. Both the Skolt Sámi and the people of Salla had experienced land loss and resettlement in the wake of the Second World War, and my plan was to compare the long-term consequences of this disruption to their lives in the two communities. As before, I gathered a lot of material, and resolved to work on it over the coming years. This resulted in a handful of articles – on the estimation of work and forms of cooperation in herding, farming and forestry, on questions of land, labour and livelihood, and on the problem of depopulation in marginal regions. For a while, I dallied with rural sociology, and in 1986 I convened an international symposium on 'The Social Implications of Agrarian Change in Northern and Eastern Finland', resulting in an eponymous volume (Ingold 1988c).

This volume was more widely reviewed than anything else I've written, simply because I personally posted a copy to all the journals I could think of. But the reviews, though positive, did nothing to save the volume from the oblivion into which it would fall. The few articles I had managed to write likewise languished unread. They had been intended as no more than preliminary sketches for the monograph I eventually planned to write, *Farmers of the Northern Forest*. But it was all to no avail. My heart just wasn't in it. My Salla research felt like an offshoot that was withering on the branch, even as I was irresistibly lured by the lofty spires of so-called 'grand theory'. I would get back to it in the end, I thought, but never imagined at the time that it would not be for another forty-odd years. Why did I not refer back to my observations from Salla in the meantime? To anyone who asked, I explained that I did not want to present material that was still, as it were, half-baked. 'Let me first write it up properly,' I would say. But of course, I never did. It remains my next project.

But I had another ambition too. It was to secure proper recognition for anthropological research in the circumpolar North.[1] This was

---

1   This circumpolar sense of North-ness should not be confused with the sense implied by what many scholars call 'the Global North', in reference to the overwhelming concentration of wealth and power in the world's northern hemisphere.

not quite the same, however, as placing the North on a par with other so-called 'ethnographic regions'. There was, I felt, something about the North, some sensibility, that upends the very idea of regionality, and even of the ethnographic as conventionally understood. The same is true, of course, of the West. But whereas the idea of the West is founded on principles of universality, progress and human ascendancy over nature, it seemed to me that a northern sensibility rests on precisely the opposite principles: of manifold difference or pluriversality, the continuity of life and human co-becoming with other inhabitants of a more-than-human world. Far from adding another ethnographic region, this sensibility, I thought, could offer a way of doing anthropology otherwise than by regional comparison: a way that would foster conversations among scholars and Indigenous peoples from around the world, in a spirit of conviviality. And so indeed it has turned out, in many exemplary collaborations involving researchers and inhabitants of lands ranging from northeastern Siberia to Alaska and everywhere in between, until cruelly cut short by the Russian invasion of Ukraine.

Many of these collaborations have been initiated and led by the University of the Arctic, a consortium of higher education institutions from around the circumpolar North. In 2007, I was invited to present a keynote address to the UArctic conference, held in Rovaniemi, the capital city of Finnish Lapland. The full and rather cumbersome title of my address was: 'Conversations from the North: scholars of many disciplines and inhabitants of many places in dialogue with one another, with animals and plants, and with the land'. This is what the North meant, and still means, to me. It is fundamentally a conversation, or rather a nexus of many conversations, embracing everyone and everything. These are literally conversations *from*, not *about*. They grow from the land, in places and along paths, just as plants and animals do. The North, then, is their breeding ground, not a platform for their enactment. It was for the same reason that in the design of the BOREAS programme – the first comprehensive, international and multidisciplinary programme in the humanities and social sciences for research among northern circumpolar peoples – we chose the title *Histories from the North*.[2]

When, in 1999, I moved to the University of Aberdeen to set up a programme focused on the Anthropology of the North, my aim was to place these conversations at the heart of our approach to teaching and research. In presenting the subject to students, our courses would reflect the principles of pluriversality, continuity and co-becoming on which they rest. As our graduate programme developed, I wanted to ensure that no research student ever faced the isolation that I did on returning from fieldwork in Lapland – not, however, by providing them with a regional identity to wear on their sleeve, but by introducing them to the very conversations in which North-ness consists. Our location, in the city of Aberdeen, played into this. Considered remote from the perspective of the so-called 'golden triangle' of Oxford, Cambridge and London, Aberdeen is itself a northern city, with long historic connections to circumpolar lands both to the east and to the west. And the University of Aberdeen, drawing on these connections, has a peculiarly northern complexion. Its history, too, is *from* the North, as is its scholarship.

That's why, in 2012, the University selected 'The North' as one of its flagship themes for multidisciplinary research. The theme, which I led for its first five years, brought together scholars from across the disciplinary spectrum, ranging from art history, through archaeology and anthropology, to geoscience. Around that time, investing in strategic research themes had become the latest fashion among university administrators, and plenty of other universities were doing the same. But our theme on 'The North' was unique. Once again, my overriding aim was to avoid closing off the North as a region, in favour of open-ended conversation. As I put it in the title of an essay first drafted for a conference at the Max Planck Institute,

---

2   The BOREAS programme, funded by the European Science Foundation, was led by Piers Vitebsky, of the Scott Polar Research Institute at the University of Cambridge, and ran from 2006 to 2009. See http://archives.esf.org/coordinating-research/euroc ores/programmes/boreas.html.

Afterword

Halle, in 2014, 'The North is Everywhere'. Unlike the everywhere of the West, usually imagined as a featureless globe upon the surface of which all life and history is enacted, the everywhere of Northness, I argued, lies in the extended web of paths woven by living creatures as they thread their ways through an ever-unfolding environment. Five years later, and after much revision, the essay was published in a volume, *Knowing from the Indigenous North*, which included several Sámi scholars among its contributors (Ingold 2019).

A couple of years previously, I had presented a draft of this essay to the anthropology seminar at the London School of Economics. The response was sceptical. My critics, suspicious of the parallels between my characterisation of the North and the approach I had already set out in books like *The Perception of the Environment* and *Being Alive*, accused me of using the North as a surrogate for a philosophy that was essentially my own. 'What do you expect?' I retorted. 'Had it not been for my own immersion in northern ways, I wouldn't be thinking along these lines in the first place.' And this is precisely the point. Like any novice anthropologist, I had begun by going over my fieldnotes, again and again. I was a stickler for detail, and found it hard to tell the wood from the trees. So long as we think of anthropological analysis as a process of sifting out generalities from the mass of specificities, holding to the middle ground is always a challenge. That's why anthropologists have so commonly found refuge in the ethnographic region, a kind of halfway house between particulars and universals, and why, initially, I had felt left out in the cold.

But discovering what I had really learned during my sojourns in Lapland took much longer, and it did not come from any analysis of the 'ethnographic facts'. Quite to the contrary, it came in the form of a radical reassessment of my whole way of doing anthropology, as a way of knowing that grows *from the inside* of our experience of doing things, of inhabiting a world – or, in a word, of being. The truth we seek, I realised, is neither particular nor general, nor halfway between the two, but has a certain resonant depth. You can feel it.

It is like the truth in music, or in art. Only as this realisation dawned did I begin to see that as a species of knowing from the inside, anthropology shares common cause not so much with science as we know it, but with fields of art, architecture and design. This would eventually culminate in the last big project I would undertake before my retirement. What was known as KFI – an acronym for 'Knowing from the Inside: Anthropology, Art, Architecture and Design' – ran from 2013 to 2018, with generous funding from the European Research Council.

In all of this, however, I never left the North. It was rather the North that had taught me that as an exploration of knowing in being, anthropology is not, in the first place, an ethnographic enterprise. Nor is it a generalising science. The motion for the first debate of GDAT held in Manchester in 1988, 'Social anthropology is a generalising science or it is nothing', had caught the tension between the alternatives of ethnographic specificity and scientific generality. But it also caught a turning point in my own intellectual life. For it was at that moment that I began to see another way for anthropology, namely, as the very web of conversations in which I was discovering the essence of North-ness. Whereas generalising from particulars is a characteristically Western gambit, the way of the North allows knowledge to grow from our vital and visceral involvements with fellow inhabitants of the lands and waters of a shared planet. For me, this turnaround was wonderfully liberating. The ethnographic homelessness I had experienced on first returning from the field could finally give way to the nomadic scholarship I have enjoyed ever since. I can now pitch my tent wherever I like!

REFERENCES

Ahmad, I. ed. 2021. *Anthropology and Ethnography are Not Equivalent: Reorienting Anthropology for the Future*. New York and Oxford: Berghahn

Aporta, C. 2004, Routes, trails and tracks: Trail breaking among the Inuit of Igloolik. *Études/Inuit/Studies*, 28(2): 9–38.

Asad, T. ed. 1973. *Anthropology and the Colonial Encounter*. London: Ithaca Press.

Barad, K. 2007. *Meeting the Universe Halfway: Quantum Physics and the Entanglement of Matter and Meaning*. Durham, NC: Duke University Press.

Barnes, J. A. 1971. *Three Styles in the Study of Kinship*. London: Tavistock.

Barth, F. 1965. *Political Leadership Among Swat Pathans*. London: Athlone Press.

Bartlett, F. C. 1992. *Remembering: A Study in Experimental and Social Psychology*. Cambridge: Cambridge University Press.

Bender, B. ed. 1993. *Landscape: Politics and Perspectives*. Oxford: Berg.

Bergson, H. 1911. *Creative Evolution* (trans. A. Mitchell). London: Macmillan.

Bernstein, N. A. 1996. On dexterity and its development (trans. M. L. Latash). In Latash, M. L. and Turvey, M. T. eds. *Dexterity and Its Development*. Mahwah, N.J.: Lawrence Erlbaum Associates, pp. 3–244.

Biesta, G. 2006. *Beyond Learning: Democratic Education for a Human Future*. Boulder, CO: Paradigm Publishers.

Biesta, G. 2013. *The Beautiful Risk of Education*. Boulder, CO: Paradigm Publishers.

Bogoras, W. G. 1904–9. *The Chukchee*. Jesup North Pacific Expeditions, vol. VII (3 parts). American Museum of Natural History Memoir 11. Leiden: E.J. Brill.

Boulter, S. 2019. *Why Medieval Philosophy Matters*. London: Bloomsbury Academic.

Chatwin, B. 1987. *The Songlines*. London: Jonathan Cape.

Chomsky, N. 1980. *Rules and Representations*. New York: Columbia University Press.

Clifford, J. and Marcus, G.E. eds. 1986. *Writing Culture: The Poetics and Politics of Anthropology.* Berkeley, CA: University of California Press.

Clutton-Brock, J. ed. 1989. *The Walking Larder: Patterns of Domestication, Pastoralism and Predation*. London: Unwin Hyman.

da Col, G. ed. 2017. Debate collection: Two or three things I love or hate about ethnography. *HAU: Journal of Ethnographic Theory* 7(1), 1–69.

Deleuze, G. and Guattari, F. 2004. *A Thousand Plateaus: Capitalism and Schizophrenia* (trans. B. Massumi). London: Continuum.

Dewey, J. 1966. *Democracy and Education: An Introduction to the Philosophy of Education*. New York: Free Press.

Ergül, H. 2017. On anthropology, education and university: An Interview with Tim Ingold. *Moment Journal* 4(1), 7–13.

Eriksen, T.H. 2015. *Fredrik Barth: An Intellectual Biography*. London: Pluto Press.

Escobar, A. 2018. *Designs for the Pluriverse: Radical Interdependence, Autonomy and the Making of Worlds*. Durham, NC: Duke University Press.

Evens, T.M.S. and Handelman, D. eds. 2006. *The Manchester School: Practice and Ethnographic Praxis in Anthropology*. New York and Oxford: Berghahn.

Ferrández, L. F. A. 2013. Ways of living: Tim Ingold on culture, biology and the anthropological task (Interview). *Revista de AntropologíaIberoamericana* 8(3), 285–302.

Geertz, C. 1963. *Agricultural Involution: the Processes of Ecological Change in Indonesia*. Berkeley, CA: University of California Press.

Gibson, J. 1979. *The Ecological Approach to Visual Perception*. Boston, Massachusetts: Houghton Mifflin.

Giddens, A. 1970. *Central Problems in Social Theory*. London: Macmillan.

Glasgow Anthropology Network. 2020. An interview with Tim Ingold. (Online, accessed 25 April 2024). Available at https://www.youtube.com/watch?v=svAPCxmDIDw.

Godelier, M. 1972. *Rationality and Irrationality in Economics* (trans. B. Pearce). London: New Left Books.

Hallam, E. and Ingold, T. eds. 2007. *Creativity and Cultural Improvisation*. Oxford: Berg.

Hallowell, A. I. 1960. Ojibwa ontology, behavior and world view. In Diamond, S. ed. *Culture in History: Essays in Honor of Paul Radin*. New York and London: Columbia University Press, pp. 19–52.

Heaney, S. 1990. *New selected poems, 1966–87*. London: Faber & Faber.

Heidegger, M. 2013. Building dwelling thinking. In Heidegger, M. *Poetry, Language, Thought* (trans. A. Hofstadter). New York: Harper Perennial, pp. 145–61.

Hicks, D. 2016. The temporality of the landscape revisited. *Norwegian Archaeological Review* 49(1), 5–22.

Hirsch, E. and O'Hanlon, M. eds. 1995. *The Anthropology of Landscape: Perspectives on Place and Space*. Oxford: Clarendon Press.

Hornborg, A. 2018. Relationism as revelation or prescription? Some thoughts on how Ingold's implicit critique of modernity could be harnessed to political ecology. *Interdisciplinary Science Reviews* 43(3–4), 253–63.

Howard, P. M. 2018. The anthropology of human-environment relations: materialism with and without Marxism. *Focaal* 82, 64–79.

Howes, D. 2022. The misperception of the environment: a critical evaluation of the work of Tim Ingold and an alternative guide to the use of the senses in anthropological theory. *Anthropological Theory* 22(4), 443–66.

Ingold, T. 1974. On reindeer and men. *Man* (N.S.) 9(4), 523–38.

Ingold, T. 1976. *The Skolt Lapps Today*. Cambridge: Cambridge University Press.

Ingold, T. 1980. *Hunters, Pastoralists and Ranchers: Reindeer*

Ingold, T. 1983. The architect and the bee: reflections on the work of animals and men. *Man* 18(1), 1–20.

Ingold, T. 1986a. *Evolution and Social Life*. New York and London: Routledge.

Ingold, T. 1986b. *The Appropriation of Nature: Essays on Human Ecology and Social Relations*. Manchester: Manchester University Press.

Ingold, T. ed. 1988a. *What is an Animal?* London: Unwin Hyman.

Ingold, T. 1988b. Introduction. In Ingold, T. ed. *What is an Animal?* London: Unwin Hyman.

Ingold, T. ed. 1988c. *The Social Implications of Agrarian Change in Northern and Eastern Finland*. Helsinki: The Finnish Anthropological Society.

Ingold, T. 1993. The temporality of the landscape. *World Archaeology* 25 (2), 152–74.

Ingold. T. 1994. From trust to domination: an alternative history of human–animal relations. In Manning, A. and Serpell, J. eds. *Animals and Human Society: Changing Perspectives*. London and New York: Routledge, pp. 1–22. (Reproduced in Ingold 2011b: 61–76.)

Ingold, T. 1996a. Preface. In Ingold, T. ed. *Key Debates in Anthropology*. London: Routledge, pp. ix–xiii.

Ingold, T. 1996b. General introduction. In Ingold, T. ed. *Key Debates in Anthropology*. London: Routledge, pp. 1–14.

Ingold, T. 1996c. Social relations, human ecology and the evolution of culture: an exploration of concepts and definitions. In Lock, A. and Peters, C. R., eds. *Handbook of Human Symbolic Evolution*. Oxford: Clarendon, pp. 178–203.

Ingold, T. 1999. 'Tools for the hand, language for the face': an appreciation of Leroi-Gourhan's *Gesture and Speech*. *Studies in History and Philosophy of Biological and Biomedical Sciences* 30(4), 411–53.

Ingold, T. 2003. Two reflections on ecological knowledge. In Sanga, G. and Ortalli, G. eds. *Nature Knowledge: Ethnoscience, Cognition and Utility*. Oxford: Berghahn, pp. 301–11.

Ingold, T. 2005. Epilogue: towards a politics of dwelling. *Conservation and Society* 3 (2), 501–8.

Ingold, T. 2006. Rethinking the animate, re-animating thought. *Ethnos* 71 (1): 9–20.

Ingold, T. 2007a. *Lines: A Brief History*. London: Routledge.

Ingold, T. 2007b. Materials against materiality. *Archaeological Dialogues* 14(1), 1–16.

Ingold, T. 2008. Anthropology is *not* ethnography. *Proceedings of the British Academy* 154, 69–92

Ingold, T. 2011a. *Being Alive: Essays on Movement, Knowledge and Description*. London: Routledge

Ingold, T. 2011b. *The Perception of the Environment: Essays on Livelihood, Dwelling and Skill*. London: Routledge (first edition published in 2000).

Ingold, T. 2013a. *Making: Anthropology, Archaeology, Art and Architecture*. London: Routledge.

Ingold, T. 2013b. Anthropology beyond humanity. *Suomen Antropologi/Journal of the Finnish Anthropology Society* 38(3), 5–23.(A revised version of this article is included in *Ingold* 2022a: 289–309.)

Ingold, T. 2014a. That's enough about ethnography. *HAU: Journal of Ethnographic Theory* 4(1), 383–95.

Ingold, T. 2014b. A life in books. *Journal of the Royal Anthropological Institute (N.S.)* 20:189–91.

Ingold, T. 2015. *The Life of Lines*. London: Routledge.

Ingold, T. 2016a. *Lines: A Brief History* (Routledge Classics Edition). London: Routledge.

Ingold, T. 2016b. Archaeology with its back to the world. *Norwegian Archaeological Review* 49(1), 30–2.

Ingold, T. 2017a. Anthropology contra ethnography. *HAU: Journal of Ethnographic Theory* 7(1), 21–6.

Ingold, T. 2017b. Taking taskscape to task. In Rajala, U. and Mills, P. eds. *Forms of Dwelling: 20 years of Taskscapes in Archaeology*. Oxford: Oxbow Books, pp. 16–27.

Ingold, T. 2017c. On human correspondence. *Journal of the Royal Anthropological Institute* (N.S.) 23, 9–27.

Ingold, T. 2018a. *Anthropology: Why It Matters*. Cambridge: Polity.

Ingold, T. 2018b. *Anthropology and/as Education*. London: Routledge.

Ingold, T. 2018c. From science to art and back again: the pendulum of an anthropologist. *Interdisciplinary Science Reviews* 43 (3–4), 213–27.

Ingold, T. 2019. The North is everywhere. In Eriksen, T. H., Valkonen, S. and Valkonen, J. eds. *Knowing from the Indigenous North: Sámi Approaches to History, Politics and Belonging*. London: Routledge, pp. 108–19.

Ingold, T. 2021a. Afterword. In Ahmad, I. ed. *Anthropology and Ethnography are Not Equivalent: Reorienting Anthropology for the Future*. New York and Oxford: Berghahn, pp. 141–52.

Ingold, T. 2021b. *Correspondences*. Cambridge: Polity.

Ingold, T. 2021c. In praise of amateurs. *Ethnos* 86 (1),153–72.

Ingold, T. 2022a. *Imagining for Real: Essays on Creation, Attention and Correspondence*. London: Routledge.

Ingold, T. ed. 2022b. *Knowing from the Inside: Cross-Disciplinary Experiments with Matters of Pedagogy*. London: Bloomsbury.

Ingold, T. 2024. *The Rise and Fall of Generation Now*. Cambridge: Polity.

Ingold, T., Riches, D. and Woodburn, J. eds. 1988. *Hunters and Gatherers, Vols I: History, Evolution and Social Change* and *II: Property, Power and Ideology*. London: Routledge.

Ingold, T. with Lucas, R. 2007. The 4 As (Anthropology, Archaeology, Art and Architecture): reflections on a teaching and learning experience. In Harris, M. ed. *Ways of Knowing: New Approaches in the Anthropology of Knowledge and Learning*. New York: Berghahn, pp. 287–305.

Ingold, T. and Lee Vergunst, J. eds. 2008. *Ways of Walking: Ethnography and Practice on Foot*. Farnham: Ashgate.

Ingold, T. and Simonetti, C. 2022. Introducing solid fluids. *Theory, Culture and Society* 39 (2), 3–29.

Interdisciplinary Science Reviews. 2018. Special issue: From science to art and back again: the anthropology of Tim Ingold, 43 (3–4): 209–378.

Jackson, M. 1989. *Paths Toward a Clearing: Radical Empiricism and Ethnographic Inquiry*. Bloomington, IN: Indiana University Press.

Jackson, M. D. 2018. Parallel lines and forking paths: reflections on the work of Tim Ingold. *Interdisciplinary Science Reviews* 43 (3–4), 317–32.

James, W. 2012. *A Pluralistic Universe* (1909), Auckland, NZ: The Floating Press.

Kaartinen, T. 2018. Interview with Tim Ingold. *Suomen Antropologi* 43 (1), 51–61.

Kochan, J. 2024. Ingold, hermeneutics and hylomorphic animism. *Anthropological Theory* 24 (1), 88–108.

Kohn, E. 2013. *How Forests Think: Toward an Anthropology Beyond the Human.* Berkeley, CA: University of California Press.

Kuper, A. 1996. *Anthropology and Anthropologists: The Modern British School* (third edition). London: Routledge.

Lave, J. 1988. *Cognition in Practice.* Cambridge: Cambridge University Press.

Lave, J. and Wenger, E. 1991. *Situated Learning: Legitimate Peripheral Participation.* Cambridge: Cambridge University Press.

Leach, E. R. 1967. *A Runaway World?* (The 1967 Reith Lectures). London: Oxford University Press.

Leroi-Gourhan, A. 1993. *Gesture and Speech* (trans. A. B. Berger). Cambridge, MA: MIT Press (first published in 1964–5).

Lye, T.-P. 1997. Knowledge, forest and hunter-gatherer movement: the Batek of Pahang, Malaysia, Unpublished doctoral dissertation, University of Hawai'i.

MacDougall, S. 2016. Enough about ethnography: an interview with Tim Ingold. *Society for Cultural Anthropology.* (Online, accessed 19 March 2024). Available at https://culanth.org/fieldsights/enough-about-ethnography-an-interview-with-tim-ingold

Marx, K. 1963. *Eighteenth Brumaire of Louis Bonaparte.* New York: International Publishers.

Marx, K. 1973. *Grundrisse* (trans. M. Nicolaus). Harmondsworth: Penguin.

Marx, K. and Engels, F. 1977. *The German Ideology,* ed. C. J. Arthur. London: Lawrence & Wishart.

Masschelein, J. 2010a. The idea of critical e-ducational research – e-ducating the gaze and inviting to go walking. In Gur-Ze'ev, I. ed. *The Possibility/Impossibility of a New Critical Language in Education.* Rotterdam: Sense Publishers, pp. 275–91.

Masschelein, J. 2010b. E-ducating the gaze: the idea of a poor pedagogy. *Ethics and Education* 5(1), 43–53.

Mauss, M. 1973. Techniques of the body (trans. B. Brewster). *Economy and Society* 2 (1), 70–88.

Merleau-Ponty, M. 1962. *Phenomenology of Perception* (trans. C. Smith). London: Routledge and Kegan Paul (first published in 1945).

Midgley, D. ed. 2005. *The essential Mary Midgley.* London: Routledge.

Midgley, M. 1978. *Beast and Man: The Roots of Human Nature.* Ithaca, NY: Cornell University Press.

Midgley, M. 1983. *Animals and Why They Matter.* Harmondsworth: Penguin.

Mills, D. 2008. *Difficult Folk?: A Political History of Social Anthropology.* Oxford: Berghahn.

Morgan, L. H. 1868. *The American Beaver and His Works.* New York: Burt Franklin.

Morphy, H. ed. 1989. *Animals into Art.* London: Unwin Hyman.

Neisser, U. and Winograd, E. eds. *Remembering Reconsidered: Ecological and Traditional Approaches to the Study of Memory.* Cambridge: Cambridge University Press.

Oyama, S. 1985. *The Ontogeny of Information: Developmental Systems and Evolution.* Cambridge: Cambridge University Press.

Pfaffenberger, B. 1988. Fetishised objects and humanised nature: towards an anthropology of technology. *Man* (N.S.) 23: 236–52.

Pfaffenberger, B. 1992. Social anthropology of technology. *Annual Review of Anthropology* 21: 491–516.

Porr, M. and Weidtmann, N. eds. 2024a. *One World Anthropology and Beyond: A Multidisciplinary Engagement with the Work of Tim Ingold.* London: Routledge.

Porr, M. and Weidtmann, N. 2024b. Acknowledgements. In Porr, M. and Weidtmann, N. eds. *One World Anthropology and Beyond: A Multidisciplinary Engagement with the Work of Tim Ingold.* London: Routledge, pp. xiii–xiv.

Porr, M., Weidtmann, N. and Ingold, T. 2024. Tim Ingold – biographical and research interview. In Porr, M. and Weidtmann, N. eds. *One World Anthropology and Beyond: A Multidisciplinary Engagement with the Work of Tim Ingold.* London: Routledge, pp. 3–11.

Radcliffe-Brown A.R. 1952. *Structure and Function in Primitive Society.* London: Cohen & West.

Rajala, U. and Mills, P. eds. *Forms of Dwelling: 20 Years of Taskscapes in Archaeology*. Oxford: Oxbow books.

Reclaiming Our University. 2016. The Manifesto. (Online, accessed 19 March 2024). Available at https://reclaimingouruniversity.wordpress.com

Rubin, D. 1988. Go for the skill. In Neisser, U. and Winograd, E. eds. *Remembering Reconsidered: Ecological and Traditional Approaches to the Study of Memory*. Cambridge: Cambridge University Press, pp. 374–82.

Sahlins, M. D. 1960. Evolution: specific and general. In Sahlins, M. D. and Service, E. R. eds. *Evolution and Culture*. Ann Arbor, MI: University of Michigan Press pp. 12–44.

Sahlins, M. D. 1972. *Stone Age Economics*. London: Tavistock.

Sahlins, M. D. 1976. *Culture and Practical Reason*. Chicago, IL: University of Chicago Press.

Searle, J. R. 1979. The intentionality of intention and action. *Inquiry* 22: 253–80.

Searle, J. R. 1984. *Minds, Brains and Science*. London: British Broadcasting Corporation.

Shryock, A. 2016. Ethnography: Provocation. Correspondences, *Fieldsights*, May 3. (Online, accessed 25 April 2024). Available at https://culanth.org/fieldsights/ethnography-provocation.

Strathern, M. 1988. *The Gender of the Gift: Problems with Women and Problems with Society in Melanesia*. Berkeley, CA: University of California Press.

Terray, E. 1972. *Marxism and 'Primitive' Societies* (trans. M. Klopper). London: Monthly Review Press.

Tilley, C. 1994. *A Phenomenology of Landscape: Places, Paths and Monuments*. Oxford: Berg.

Tilley, C. 2007. Materiality in materials. *Archaeological Dialogues* 14 (1), 16–20.

Uexküll, J. von 2010. *A Foray into the Worlds of Animals and Humans, with A theory of Meaning* (trans. J. D. O'Neil). Minneapolis, MN: University of Minnesota Press.

Wagner, R. 2016. *The Invention of Culture* (second edition, with a new foreword by T. Ingold). Chicago, IL: University of Chicago Press.

Weiner, J. 1991. *The Empty Place: Poetry, Space and Being Among*

the Foi of Papua New Guinea. Bloomington, IN: Indiana University Press.
Weiner, J. 2001. *Tree Leaf Talk: A Heideggerian Anthropology*. London: Routledge.
Whitehead, A. N. 1926. *Science and the Modern World: Lowell Lectures 1925*. Cambridge: Cambridge University Press.
Whitehead, A. N. 1929. *Process and Reality: An Essay in Cosmology*. Cambridge: Cambridge University Press.
Willis, R. ed. 1990. *Signifying Animals: Human Meaning in the Natural World*. London: Unwin Hyman.
Wilson, E. O. 1975. *Sociobiology: The New Synthesis*. Cambridge, MA: Belknap Press of Harvard University Press.

INDEX

Aberdeen, University of 10, 50, 207
   'Anthropology of the North' programme at 54, 207
   Department of Anthropology 7, 50–9, 73, 170
   'Reclaiming Our University' Movement 11, 95–9
   supervision of doctoral students at 53–4
   undergraduate teaching at 53
   see also circumpolar North, anthropological research in
academia, colonial legacy in 4, 11, 70–2
academic career
   see Aberdeen, University of; Manchester, University of
animals
   see human–animal relations
anthropocentrism 7, 115–17
   and environmental sustainability 117
anthropology
   challenges facing 4, 73, 166, 188–91, 208
   colonial legacies and 4, 70–2
   decolonising of 72–3
   distinctiveness of 5, 94–5, 103
   as education 5–6, 9, 72, 88–93, 183–4
   and 'ethnographic regions' 44, 203–6
   history of 4, 43, 55, 169
   beyond humanity 7, 141–2, 147–9
   importance of 190–1
   for one world 7, 165–7
   professionalisation of 12, 70, 84
   public profile of 4, 11–12, 78–80, 188–90
   as subject to study 24–5, 93–4
   synthesis of with other fields 57, 102–3, 175–7
   see also archaeology; architecture; art; ethnography; fieldwork; 4As course; participant observation; sociology; social sciences; teaching; theory; writing

Anthropology and/as Education (2018) 5–6, 90–2
Anthropology: Why it Matters (2018) 5–6, 93
Appropriation of Nature (1986), *The* 9, 44–5
archaeology
   and anthropology 7, 25, 58, 176, 183, 207
   and landscape 105
   and taskscape 108
architecture 54, 57, 59, 183, 199
art 22, 54, 57–9, 162, 183, 199
history 105–6, 108, 118, 207

Barnes, John 12, 27–8, 36–7
Barth, Fredrik 8, 26, 28–9, 178–81
   see also transactionalism
Being Alive (2011) 58, 170, 200, 208
belief, religious 7, 167–9
   and faith 168
Bergson, Henri 8, 45, 47, 89, 105, 165
Biesta, Gert 90–1
biodiversity 74–5
biology 44, 45–6, 102, 130–1, 148–9
   and culture 3, 45, 130–31
   Darwinian and neo-Darwinian 11, 45, 67, 102, 132–3, 169
   developmental 57, 103
   evolutionary 9, 45–7, 89
   and sociobiology 46
BOREAS programme, see circumpolar North, anthropological research in

Cambridge, University of 28, 39, 207
   Department of Social Anthropology 25–7, 50
   doctoral research at 26, 27–30, 204
   undergraduate studies at 23–6, 74, 90, 176
   see also Barnes, John; fieldwork; Hart, Keith; Leach, Edmund; writing
childhood experiences and influences 18–22
   secondary education 19–20
   father's work as mycologist 20–2
   first trip to Finland 23
circumpolar North, anthropological research in 43–4, 55, 80, 138, 204–7
   BOREAS programme 206–7
climate crisis 116–17
colonialism 37, 72, 150, 185, 186
correspondence 160–2, 167
   versus interaction 161
   versus intra-action 161
   meaning of 160
creation 163–5
   versus creativity 164
   and generations 164–5
   meaning of 164
culture
   and biology 3, 45, 130–1

and diversity 73–4
and skill 130–1
see also material culture

democracy 68
  and education, Dewey on 98
Dewey, John 9, 68, 88–90, 98
diversity
  biodiversity 74–5
  cultural 73–4
  and difference 73
doctoral research
  see Cambridge, University of
dwelling
  versus habitation 108–9
  Heidegger on 48, 109
  meaning of 109, 128
  poetics of 110
  and producing 128
dwelling perspective 7, 105–8
  and landscape 106–7
  and taskscape 107–8

ecology 45, 46, 106
  and anthropology 44–5, 48
  see also Appropriation of Nature (1986), The
education
  and curiosity 133
  rather than ethnography, as purpose of anthropology 91, 183–4
  and fieldwork 33–4, 71, 91, 183
  meaning of 90–1
  sensory 158–60
  and teaching 6–7, 9, 92, 159–60, 181–4
  transmission model of 90
  as a way of leading life 90, 159
  see also Anthropology and/as Education (2018); Biesta, Gert; Dewey, John; higher education; learning; Masschelein, Jan; teaching
environment
  and anthropocentrism 116–17
  concept of 104
  versus landscape 105–8
  see also Appropriation of Nature (1986), The; Manchester, University of, undergraduate teaching at; Perception of the Environment (2000), The; Uexküll, Jakob von
ESRC (Economic and Social Research Council) 27
ethnography 14, 157, 171, 195
  versus anthropology 4, 11–12, 72–2, 75–88, 190
  and colonial legacy 72
  versus education 91, 183–4
  multi-species 141, 147–9
  see also anthropology; fieldnotes; fieldwork; participant observation; writing
evolution 44–7, 151, 164
  versus history 3, 45, 130, 169
  see also biology

Evolution and Social Life (1986) 9, 44–7, 127

fieldnotes 76–7, 82, 171, 193, 208
  importance of 86–8
  writing of 12, 36–7, 87
fieldwork, anthropological 26, 29–30, 71–2, 82, 86–8, 203–9
  doctoral research with Skolt Sámi (northeastern Finland) 12–13, 27, 31–6, 41, 195
  versus ethnography 75–8
  importance of 34, 91
  language learning and 12, 30–1
  plans for future 14, 171
  research in Salla (eastern Lapland) 14, 44, 52, 171
  and teaching 83, 183
  transformative nature of 33, 91
  see also ethnography; fieldnotes; research; writing
Finland 12, 23, 26–7, 32–6, 195, 203
4As course (Anthropology, Archaeology, Art and Architecture) 183–4
fungi 18, 20–2, 104
  see also the mycelial person, concept of

GDAT (Group for Debates in Anthropological Theory) 63–4, 209

generations, entwinement of 14, 171
  see also Rise and Fall of Generation Now (2024), *The*
Gibson, James 8, 9, 47–8, 124, 179
Godelier, Maurice 45, 127, 178–80

Hart, Keith 8, 25, 40–3
Heidegger, Martin 48, 109, 128
Hicks, Dan 113–14
higher education
  and neoliberalism 98
  purpose of 97–8
  'Reclaiming Our University' Movement 11, 95–9
  REF (Research Excellence Framework) 170
history 44–5, 124, 167–70
  cultural 51–2
  versus evolution 45, 130, 169
  of notation 153–5
human–animal relations 7, 43, 138–49
  domestication 145–7
  multi-species ethnography 141, 147–9
  as social relations 138, 140–1
  trust vs domination 140–1, 146–7
  see also anthropology, beyond humanity; language; Midgley, Mary
humaning 148
humanities 93, 99, 106, 166, 197, 206

see *also* natural sciences, versus humanities
humanity 162, 197–8
  concept of 119
  and nature 119, 120
  unsliced 4, 95, 103
  see *also* anthropology, beyond humanity
hunter-gatherer studies 45, 59, 140, 147, 180

imagination, versus reality 3, 7, 162–3
Imagining for Real (2022) 2, 138, 147, 162–70
Ingold, Anna 27, 30, 186
interviews 17–18

landscape 22, 156, 158, 195–6
  anthropological approach to 105–8
  meaning of 106
  northern 13, 31–2, 33–5, 157–8
  perception of 110–12
  versus taskscape 106–8
  temporality of 106, 113–14
language 130, 143–5, 163
  and academic writing 67, 118–19, 198
  languaging, concept of 144–5
  see *also* fieldwork, language learning and
Lave, Jean 182–3
Leach, Edmund 25–6, 74, 90, 191
learning
  anthropological studies of 182
  and education 5
  and fieldwork 33–4, 52, 71, 82, 91, 183
  from PhD students 9, 180–1, 191–3
  and skill 66, 111–12, 126
  and wisdom 5–6, 93, 98
  see *also* fieldwork, language learning and; Lave, Jean; teaching
Leroi-Gourhan, André 8, 89–90, 151–2, 154–5, 179
life
  education as a way of leading 90, 159
  and generations 1, 117, 164, 171
  as movement 115, 151, 156–60
  social 70, 73–4, 107, 139
  see *also* lines
lines 8–9, 13, 21–2, 34, 58–9, 104
  history and anthropology of 149–52, 156–60
  lifelines 156
  and anthropology of literacy 153–5
  and history of notation 153–5
  threads vs traces 152–3
Lines: A Brief History (2007) 9, 58, 156

Manchester, University of
  Department of Social Anthropology 38–42, 46, 49–50, 55, 194, 203–4

supervision of doctoral
    students at 40-1, 43, 57
  undergraduate teaching at
    43-4, 45-6, 106-7, 123, 127
Marx, Karl 8, 70, 126-8, 142, 169
Masschelein, Jan 90-1
material culture 81, 119-21,
    197-8
  see also culture
materialism, new 118-19, 197-8
materiality 7, 117-23
  versus materials 10, 118-23
Mauss, Marcel 43, 89, 150
Merleau-Ponty, Maurice 8,
    48-9, 89, 179
Midgley, Mary 139-40
modernity, Western 129-30, 150
  dissolving dichotomies of 3,
    11, 130-1
the mycelial person, concept of
    7, 8, 103-4
  and lines 104
  influenced by father's work
    as mycologist 8, 20-2, 104
  see also fungi
mycology
  see fungi; the mycelial
    person, concept of

natural sciences, versus human-
    ities 4, 106, 139, 175
neoliberalism 11
  and higher education 98

ontogeny 89
ontological turn 197-8
Oyama, Susan 8, 89

participant observation
  and ethnography 11-12,
    78-9
  and method 83-5
  as ontological commitment
    83-4
  and teaching 83
  see also anthropology;
    ethnography; fieldnotes;
    fieldwork
perception
  ecological approach to 89,
    126
  environmental 54
  Gibson on 47-8, 89
  and imagination 162-3
  Merleau-Ponty on 48-9,
    89
  see also skill
Perception of the Environment
    (2000), The 57-8, 101-3,
    126-33, 156, 162, 208
phenomenology 47-9, 57, 89,
    102-3
  see also Merleau-Ponty,
    Maurice
philosophy 94, 102, 118, 165-9,
    192
politics 10-11, 22, 66-8, 195
  as dialogue 65, 68
  democratic 68
  meaning of 65, 68
  and theory 65
  and the act of writing 10-11,
    65, 66-7
posthumanism 148, 197-8
psychology 71, 102

ecological 2, 47–8, 57, 103, 124–5, 179
  cognitive 111–12, 164
  see also Gibson, James

REF (Research Excellence Framework), see higher education
religion, see belief, religious
research
  funding 27, 67, 85, 209
  and method 83–5
  training 12, 29–30, 38, 83
  see also circumpolar North, anthropological research in; fieldwork; participant observation
Rise and Fall of Generation Now (2024), The 2, 14, 171
Rubin, David 111–12

skill 66, 111–12, 123–33
  as coordination of perception and action 124–6
  ecological approach to 125–6
  and knowledge 125
  see also techniques; technology
Skolt Lapps Today (1976), The 13, 138, 204
Skolt Sámi 12–13, 27, 30–6, 138, 195, 203–5
social anthropology, see anthropology
social sciences 93, 99, 103–4, 141–2, 197, 206

sociology 4, 28, 51, 53–5, 94–5, 142, 169
storytelling 31, 158, 195
  as a form of wayfaring 158–60
Strathern, Marilyn 44, 49–50
structural-functionalism 25–6, 69
structuralism 25

teaching
  approach to 6–7, 9, 92, 181–5, 207
  as essential part of doing anthropology 6, 183–4
  and cultivation of curiosity 133
  practice of 83–4
  standard model of 181
  see also Aberdeen, University of; anthropology; learning; Manchester, University of
techniques 124, 126
  anthropological approaches to 151, 179
technology 124, 151, 181
  anthropological approaches to 43–4, 89, 123–4
  see also skill
theory 63–5, 67, 69–70, 104–5, 178, 196, 205
  in anthropology 90, 102, 179
  as political 65
  as thinking 64
  see also GDAT
Tilley, Christopher 120–3
transactionalism 26, 29, 178

Index

Uexküll, Jakob von 142, 149
universities, see Aberdeen, University of; academia; Cambridge, University of; higher education; Manchester, University of

Werbner, Pnina 40–1
Whitehead, Alfred North 45, 47, 131

writing
 approaches to 11, 193–5
 fieldnotes 86–8
 history of 153–5
 as political 10–11, 65, 66–7
 types of writing 76–8, 81–2, 198
 writing up after fieldwork 33–4, 39
 see also ethnography; fieldnotes; lines

www.ingramcontent.com/pod-product-compliance
Lightning Source LLC
Chambersburg PA
CBHW031147020426
42333CB00013B/552